EXPERIENTIAL CIVIC LEARNING:

Construction of Models & Assessment

EXPERIENTIAL CIVIC LEARNING:

Construction of Models & Assessment

Mary L. Lo Re, Ph.D.
Wagner College

NA

NorthAmerican
Business Press
Atlanta – Seattle – South Florida - Toronto

North American Business Press, Inc

Atlanta, Georgia
Seattle, Washington
South Florida
Toronto, Canada

Experiential Civic Learning: Construction of Models and Assessment
ISBN: 978-0-9828434-5-1
© 2012 All Rights Reserved.

Along with trade books for various business disciplines, the North American Business Press also publishes a variety of academic-peer reviewed journals.

Library of Congress Control Number: 2012937354

Library of Congress
Cataloging in Publication Division
101 Independence Ave., SE
Washington, DC 20540-4320
Printed in theUnited States of America

First Edition

Dedication

This book is dedicated to the faculty in the Department of Business Administration and the Administration at Wagner College which introduced me to this field of research and supports my efforts. A special debt of gratitude goes to Dr. Anne Love who patiently read and made suggestions to the early draft of the manuscript; and to my family for their loving encouragement.

About the Author

Dr. Mary L. Lo Re, Chair of the Department of Business Administration at Wagner College, teaches statistical modeling, managerial economics, and varied finance undergraduate and graduate courses. She obtained her Ph.D. from CUNY Graduate Center specializing in Monetary Theories & Policies and International Trade. She has written and obtained several external and internal grants; received numerous newspaper, other media, community, and student involvement mentions; and presented and published in the areas of civic engagement, best practices such as writing across the curriculum, EU/EMU convergence and the economic financial crisis. Prior to academia, Dr. Lo Re obtained 17 years of practical business experience, including nine years in computer technology and eight years in upper/executive management. The author can be contacted at: mlore@wagner.edu

Preface

Experiential Civic Learning—Construction of Models & Assessment is a compact but all-inclusive essential resource guide for faculty, departments, and administrators who wish to partake in this curricula initiative and address the challenge of producing a more skilled, ethical, and civically engaged student citizen.

This book provides the background literature, rationale, practicalities, guidance, and new resources for all the phases of this learning initiative: the different modalities of experiential learning; funding and grants; considerations, construction and implementation of a single and departmental civic engagement series of courses; new rubrics to create a formal/direct and informal/indirect assessment plan; relating scores to grades; closing the learning-assessment loop.

Contents

Chapter 4: Departmental Civic Engagement Model *43*

Chapter 7: Final Considerations   *95*

References   *105*

Introduction

In academia, experiential learning, service-learning, and civic engagement have become common-place terms. While differences exist in their meaning, expectations, and deliverables, the field is growing and, in response, many institutions of higher education around the world have embraced and adopted these learning practices. Many conferences, workshops, published articles, manuscripts, and on-line resources are available to share, advance, and support this relatively new field. In fact, many organizations such as the American Association of Community Colleges, the American Association for Higher Education, the Association of American Colleges and Universities, the Carnegie Endowment for Teaching and Learning, Campus Compact, the League for Innovation, and the New American Colleges & Universities:

> ...have challenged America's colleges and universities to make student learning central to the academic mission of higher education. Those who have accepted this challenge have found service-learning to be a powerful strategy for engaging their students in mastery of academic skills and content through service to their communities. (Jones, 2003, p. 1)

Results from Campus Compact's 2010 member survey reveals that campuses that are committed to preparing students for democratic participation and are applying resources to address their communities' needs have increased to over 1,100 colleges and universities in the U.S. — a growth of 70% since 2000. Their findings show that across all institutional types, the spectrum of student participation in service-learning activities, with some schools at 100%, is wide; but, on average, 35% of students engage in service activities and spend an average of 3.7 hours per week on these activities. Furthermore, these interests are not limited to just students; faculty engagement is also quite significant. Among Campus Compact's responding schools, 93% reported offering service-learning courses during the 2009–2010 academic year. This translates to an average of 35 faculty members per campus, or 7% of all faculty. (Campus Compact, 2010)

Additionally, the National Task Force on Civic Learning and Democratic Engagement in their book, <u>A Crucible Moment: College Learning and Democracy's Future,</u> "calls for investing on a massive scale in higher education's capacity to renew this nation's social, intellectual, and civic capital." (The National Task Force on Civic Learning and Democratic Engagement, 2012) During his January 10, 2012 speech at the White House, Dr. Guarasci, one of 11 national higher education leaders on the National Task Force on Civic Learning and Democratic Engagement, emphasized this point:

> Our goal here is to do three things. First, to fundamentally increase learning in the disciplines for our students; increase their civic learning—what it means to be connected to publics they will serve in the professions they choose—and, finally, that we are actually changing things in a community, that there is an impact in those areas where we are focusing our attention. (Guarasci, 2012)

This book, *Experiential Civic Learning—Construction of Models & Assessment*, is a compact but all-inclusive resource guide for faculty, departments, and administrators in higher education at all levels and in all disciplines, that can be used to develop, implement, and assess experiential civic engagement from an individual course to a departmental level series of courses. This book is unique as it provides both the background literature as well as the rationale, practicalities, and guidance for all the phases of this learning initiative and includes new resources: the different modalities of experiential learning, funding considerations and resources, the construction of a civic engagement course, the construction a departmental civic engagement series of courses (including the considerations in constructing and implementing these initiatives), and the assessment process: how to informally and formally assess the initiatives.

In addition to guiding faculty work through the "nuts and bolts" issues related to experiential civic learning and providing the necessary resources, this book has another goal: to encourage more faculty members to partake in this curricula initiative and collaboratively address the challenge of producing a more skilled, ethical, and civically engaged student citizen.

How to Use This Book

The book is divided into seven chapters.

Chapter 1 chronicles how traditional classroom learning has evolved to include outside-the-classroom experiences. It offers a definition, a brief literature review, and the rationale and benefits of each learning modality, which will serve as the basis for the rest of the chapters in the discussion and construction of experiential civic models: reflection, service-learning, civic engagement, and learning communities. This chapter concludes with a comprehensive model—the incorporation of the above learning modalities into one course.

Chapter 2 is a brief but important topic on project funding and grants. It explores the question of whether funding is needed; the budget; funding proposal considerations; and proceeds to explore the process in obtaining funding. Twelve sources for grant opportunities are made available for your ready use.

Chapter 3 is devoted to the development of a single course experiential civic learning model. It includes a discussion on the challenges and considerations in the construction of a community-based civic engagement course; the importance of a mutual support system; changes in pedagogy and epistemology; the integration of civic engagement in a traditional course; and offers two examples of the experiential civic learning model— one initiative emanating from an Institutional grant, and another from an Instructor-written grant — with information from considerations in selection and changes to courses, partners, curriculum, project, and student and faculty deliverables. In addition, to serve as a guide and reminder, this chapter includes a "To-Do" checklist of activities that should take place before, during, and after the course or project ends. Lessons learned from educators undertaking these initiatives conclude this chapter.

Chapter 4 builds upon the discussions in the prior chapter and is dedicated to the construction and implementation of a departmental civic engagement model. It includes a discussion on the considerations in creating a departmental civic engagement initiative; the selection of its structure, the number of courses to be part of this initiative, and the number of student experiential hours; whether to use a single or multiple community partners; student-community goals, project and experiences; an example of a departmental initiative with a single community partner utilizing sequenced and different-field courses; and the advantages to the faculty in creating and participating in a collaborative departmental civic engagement program. A Departmental Course Creation Worksheet is included for ready-reference and use.

In Chapter 5, the views, definition and challenges of assessment as well as the tools of indirect assessment are reported. Considerations and the construction of an indirect assessment plan built around individual and departmental learning goals for the exemplars given in Chapters 3 and 4 are explored. Included is the sample "Civic Engagement Assessment Questionnaire" utilized in assessing the exemplar projects. A recap of Miller & Leskes' Assessment on Five Levels is next offered. Lastly, the considerations in obtaining permission to publish quotes and/or data are discussed, and a sample Permission/Release Form is offered for ready reference.

Chapter 6 is devoted to direct assessment. It is divided into two sections: constructing and assessing an individual experiential course; and assessing a departmental experiential system of courses. Specifically, Section I discusses: the definition of formal or direct assessment, considerations in constructing and assessing an experiential project, rubrics for assessing critical and civic thinking. An assessment plan for a single civic engagement project by utilizing one of the following: a reflection paper, research paper, or an oral presentation as the only source of assessment and applying rubrics for assessing content, writing, oral presentations is shown. An assessment plan utilizing multiple measurements of assessment is also offered. The materials in this section, except for the critical and civic thinking taxonomy, are new constructions. Section II uses the tools and rubrics discussed in Section I and offers a methodology in which to summarize assessment scores of individual courses into one departmental assessment rubric.

In Chapter 7, the first part of the chapter relates experiential activity, assessment scores and course grades; and shows a methodology of how to convert assessment scores to students' course grades. The second part of the chapter discusses the importance of "closing the assessment-learning loop"—incorporating assessment results into your courses—as well as offers the steps to the assessment process. Final thoughts on this topic conclude the chapter.

These chapters can be read sequentially or in isolation. As this is a resource book, please feel free to skip to the chapters or headings that attract your attention or can best meet your interests and needs.

Chapter 1

The Expansion of Experiential Learning

This Chapter Contains:

TRADITIONAL CLASSROOM TO EXPERIENTIAL LEARNING
REFLECTION
SERVICE-LEARNING
CIVIC ENGAGEMENT
LEARNING COMMUNITIES
PUTTING IT ALL TOGETHER—A COMPREHENSIVE MODEL

TRADITIONAL CLASSROOM TO EXPERIENTIAL LEARNING

In higher education, classroom learning continues to evolve from what Freire (1970) referred to as the banking method of education—where the instructor deposits information into the students' brains; and from what Coleman (1976) referred to as classroom learning which purely focuses on symbolic or information assimilation. "Deliberate" learning—learning which is intentional and where the students know they are learning; learning with a specific goal(s), as opposed to generalized learning, with a portion of this type of learning taking place outside of the classroom (Tough 1979) —is the new order.

"Students learn firsthand how experts think about and solve problems by interacting with faculty members inside and outside of the classroom. As a result, their teachers become role models, mentors, and guides for continuous, lifelong learning." (National Survey of Student Engagement)

So, in recent years, how have colleges responded to this new order? Service-learning, experiential learning, publicly engaged learning, and civic engagement are common-place terms in today's educational system. According to Imagining America, *a Resource on Promotion and Tenure in the Arts, Humanities, and Design,* "one should recognize that research, teaching, and community outreach often overlap." (p. 26) As such, service-learning, civic engagement, or, experiential/publicly engaged academic work, can be defined as:

5

...scholarly or creative activity integral to a faculty member's academic area. It encompasses different forms of making knowledge about, for, and with diverse publics and communities. Through a coherent, purposeful sequence of activities, it contributes to the public good and yields artifacts of public and intellectual value. (Eatman, 2008, p. 26)

Many models and activities have emerged to offer the students: a taste of the real world and interconnectivity; a chance to reflect; the ability to witness the imperfections and incompleteness of the models and frameworks they read in their textbooks; a deeper engagement of civic/public issues; and an opportunity to form a deeper self understanding. These characteristics, in parts, have been manifested in reflective practices, service-learning, and civic engagement in stand-alone courses; within learning communities; and/or as part of a departmental initiative. However, a distinction in the literature exists amongst the service-learning and civic engagement modalities.

What follows are the definitions, rationale, and benefits of reflection, service-learning, civic engagement, and learning communities as well as their inter-connections. This chapter serves as a precursor to the experiential civic engagement exemplar initiatives fully developed in Chapters 3 and 4.

REFLECTION

What is reflection and why should we reflect?

There is no doubt that the father of reflection is John Dewey. Dewey (1916) defines reflection as "a process which perceives connections and links between the parts of an experience" (in Boud, p. 25); or "...a form of response of the learner to an experience." (Boud, 1985, p. 18) In the context of learning, it is considered a generic term for "those intellectual and effective activities in which individuals engage to explore their experiences in order to lead to new understandings and appreciations." (Boud, 1985, p. 19) Additionally, Boyd and Fales (1983) define reflection as: "The individual experiences a 'coming together' or creative synthesis of various bits of the information previously taken in, and the formation of a new 'solution' or change in the self – what might be called a new gestalt." (p. 110)

In his later works, Dewey (1933) further expanded on reflection and defined reflective thought as "active, persistent, and careful consideration of any belief or supposed form of knowledge in the light of the grounds that support it and further conclusions to which it leads...it includes a conscious and voluntary effort to establish belief upon a firm basis of evidence and rationality." (p. 9)

In recent times, educators use reflection to heighten intellectual discourse on course material, public opinion, and out-of-classroom learning. The modes instructors employ to expand upon these efforts include assigning short papers, journaling, blogs and discussion boards, and carving out classroom time for reflective thought. While reflection may take place in isolation or in association with others, it is reflection with the association with others that is of heightened concern to educators. (Boud, 1985) However, you should note that while the instructor may be comfortable in leading a discussion on reflection, not all students are conditioned to be reflective, nor are they comfortable in explicating their reflective thoughts. Therefore, coaching on the part of the instructor is required for reflection and for this type of learning to take place inside and outside of the classroom. Faculty members that employ reflective practices will concur with Schön (1987) that those that receive real-time coaching and encouragement to reflect or think carefully about what they do while they are doing it, learn in a more profound way. In fact, the current National Survey of Student Engagement (NSSE) data support reflective practices to increase student learning.

NSSE 2010 data, by top and bottom curricular peer interaction quartiles, show comparisons of the overall percentage of first-year students who participated in reflective learning—investigating one's own thinking and applying new knowledge to one's life—in three categories: 74% vs. 38% of top and bottom curricular peer interaction quartiles of first-year students examine the strengths and weaknesses of their own views; 82% vs. 48% try to better understand the views of others; and 86% vs. 49% learn something that changed the way they understood an issue. For these same three categories, compared to seniors in all other majors, senior psychology students had an increased average percentage difference of 4%, 7%, and 6% respectively. (National Survey of Student Engagement)

In a course tied to an experiential component, reflection as a pedagogy is critical. Jones (2003) says it best when he argues that "the educational context for the service activity requires students to reflect upon their service experiences in relation to community principles, civic ideals, and universal virtues, as well as course content." (p. 2)

SERVICE-LEARNING

In higher education, modern ideas about the integration of service and learning are shaped by the early writings of John Dewey, who affirmed that better learning occurs when students have the opportunity to put into practice, in an effort to reinforce, the ideas that they are learning in the classroom. (Dewey, 1944)

So, how can we define service-learning? Is it tied with reflection? Will this require the faculty to make changes in pedagogy and/or in epistemology? Does it really produce better student learners?

Service-learning can be defined as an academic study closely tied to community service through structured reflection. This type of learning connects thought and feeling in an "intentional way" creating a framework in which students can explore how they feel about what they are thinking and what they think about how they feel. Through guided reflection, service-learning offers students opportunities to explore the relationship between their academic learning and their civic values and commitments. (Ehrlich T., 2000)

More than forty years after Dewey, other educators have begun to further explore this type of learning. The increased attention to service-learning is part of a heightened focus on engaged teaching and learning practices with scholars and academic leaders such as: the late Ernest Boyer, most noted for creating a dialogue between teachers and administrators about teaching methods and programs; John Barr and Robert Tagg, most noted for professing that the purpose of higher education is student learning and not merely providing instruction; George Kuh, most noted for his high-impact educational practices; and Terry O'Banion, noted as one of the leading spokespersons in the country on "Learning Revolution".

The heightened attention to this modality is supported by data. According to the 2010 NSSE data, 38% of first-year students in public institutions have participated in service-learning activities, and this percentage increases to 48% for private institutions. For seniors, these percentages further increase from 46% to 54% for public and private institutions, respectively. (National Survey of Student Engagement)

However, in conducting an effective service-learning course, changes in pedagogy and in epistemology are required. Jones (2003) states that adopting a service-learning component to a course not only raises issues of pedagogy but also raises issues related to what to teach (epistemology). "This is because service-learning shifts the authority of knowledge in the classroom and intentionally places community in the center of the learning process."(p. 1) Therefore, for engagement to occur, educational design is critical. Furthermore, he argues that service as academic work "assumes that cognitive, affective, and moral growths are inseparable, and that a student's ability to analyze situations and material is critical to his or her ability to make responsible decisions outside of the classroom."(p. 1)

Similar to employing the pedagogy of reflection, "service-learning is inevitably unpredictable and often uncomfortable. It challenges faculty and students on many levels as it incorporates shifting dialogues and actively engages participants in issues such as equity, difference, inclusion, tolerance, justice, and power." (Jones, 2003, p. 1)

In recent years, other service-learning champions have emerged and espouse how service-learning enhances traditional class-room learning in a variety of ways. In Furco (1996), he posits that service-learning should "...ensure equal focus on both the service being provided and the learning that is occurring." (p. 3) It is this combination of factors that distinguishes service-learning from other experiential modalities such as internships, which are designed primarily to benefit the student, and volunteerism designed to primarily benefit the community. In fact, unlike internships and other practica, service-learning "instills in students a profound understanding of community responsibility." (Tucker, McCarthy, Hoxmeier & Lenk, 1998)

Additionally, Robert A. Rhoads (1997) explores what we can learn from student involvement in community service that sheds light on how higher educational learning might be structured to involve an encounter between the self and the other, and restructured around an ethic of care. Jones (2003) states that: "Service-learning offers students an opportunity to explore the connections between the theoretical realm of the classroom and the practical needs of the community. It simultaneously reinforces the skills of critical thinking, public discourse, collective activity, and community building." He further argues that "perhaps the most important long-term benefit of service-learning is the opportunity for students to connect to a community and identify their civic roles in that community." (p. 2) Furthermore, Buddensick & Lo Re (2010) showed that students enrolled in service-learning courses have enhanced student awareness not only of themselves, but also of their communities, as well as promoted student inquiry of broader global and social issues. It is in the fulfillment of these goals that service-learning models far surpass other experiential modalities and activities.

CIVIC ENGAGEMENT

Civic engagement can be dated back to Jane Addams, a social and political activist, an author and lecturer, a community organizer, a public intellectual, and a 1931 Nobel Peace Prize recipient who emphasized that we have a special responsibility to clean up our communities and make them better places to live. But, what is civic engagement and is it synonymous with service-learning? Many new-comers to this field use these terms interchangeably; however, a distinction exists in the literature.

Civic engagement is a broader motif encompassing, but not limited to, service-learning. It has been defined as "individual and collective actions designed to identify and address issues of public concern." (Ehrlich, 2000, p. 403) As Thomas Ehrlich would echo, community engagement activities teach students "to make a difference in the civic life of our communities and develop the combination of knowledge, skills, values and motivation to make that difference" (p. 404). Civic engagement can take many forms, from individual voluntarism to organizational involvement. It can include efforts to directly address an issue or work with others in a community to solve a problem, and it can encompass a range of specific activities.

Rudolph (1990) posits that in the United States, part of the mission of higher education is to educate students for civic engagement and responsible citizenship. Jones (2003) submits that "in both civic and intellectual life one must consistently reflect on one's position, reconcile one's preconceptions with the lived experiences of others, and uphold an ethic of personal accountability and social responsibility."(p. 2) In fact, in many studies, community collaborators have stated that they value service-learning/civic engagement partnerships because they bring additional resources to the organizations and provide the opportunity to educate future professionals and community citizens (Basinger & Bartholomew, 2006; Gelmon, Holland, Seifer, Shinnamon, & Connors, 1998a; Gelmon, Holland, & Shinnamon, 1998b; Leiderman, Furco, Zapf, & Goss, 2003; Seifer & Vaughn, 2004). Furthermore, students who are engaged in civic activities "gain more in ethical development and contribute more to the welfare of their communities. Participating in civic activities also develops habits that will lead students to continue participating in civic life." (NSSE, 2011, p. 8)

Recently, institutions of higher education have received much disparagement in terms of what is being taught, or more importantly, what is not being taught. Then in 2006, the Secretary of Education Margaret Spellings commissioned "A Test of Leadership Charting the Future of U.S. Higher Education" study. The report found the following:

- "The quality of student learning at U.S. colleges and universities is inadequate and, in some cases, declining," and these shortcomings, have real-world consequences. (p. 3)

- "Employers report repeatedly that many new graduates they hire are not prepared to work, lacking the critical thinking, writing and problem-solving skills needed in today's workplaces," (p. 3) and "lack the new set of skills necessary for successful employment and continuous career development." (p. 13)

- "Institutions as well as government agencies have failed to sustain and nurture innovation in our colleges and universities." (p. 15)

While there is still much to be done to address the concerns of society expressed in the media of what we are teaching our college students, the civic engagement modality responds to higher-education's imperative to instill civic responsibility as well as the overall critique that book knowledge fails to expose students to the complexities of life.

Thus, civic engagement goes beyond Bringle & Hatcher's (1996) service-learning model to deliver a course with an experiential component with the objectives to have: (1) a further understanding of course content; (2) a broader appreciation of the discipline; and (3) an enhanced sense of civic responsibility. Civic engagement allows students to go beyond being civically aware; it allows students to actively engage-in or take-on a topic or topics that concern the public at large. Lo Re, et.al. (2011) argue that civic engagement is a superior model to service-learning in the sense that civic engagement "not only heightens the effect of civic awareness and responsibility, but also civically engages the students on an issue or issues of public concern." (2011, p. 80)

It is in the strength of this type of modality to which the examples in Chapters 3 and 4 are devoted.

LEARNING COMMUNITIES

The origin of learning communities dates back to 1928 when Alexander Meiklejohn, philosopher and advocate of free speech, formed the two-year Experimental College at the University of Wisconsin. During the first full-year of study, the curriculum stressed Greek civilization while the second year's curriculum stressed the civilization of England. Even though the "experimental college inspired its students… [it] was an administrative failure and ended in 1932." (Encyclopedia Brunoniana, 1993)

How can we define a learning community? Is it related to reflection? Does it have (or is it required for) a service, civic engagement and/or experiential component (initiative)? According to Smith, et.al. (2004), a learning community is defined as:

> a variety of curricular approaches that intentionally link or cluster two or more courses, often around an interdisciplinary theme or problem, and enrolls a common cohort of students. This represents an intentional restructuring of students' time, credit, and learning experiences to build community, enhance learning, and foster

11

connections among students, faculty, and disciplines. At their best, learning communities practice pedagogies of active engagement and reflection. (p. 67)

Additionally, according to Price (2005), learning communities are "the pedagogical embodiment of the belief that teaching and learning are relational processes, involving co-creating knowledge through relationships among students, between students and teachers, and through the environment in which these relationships operate." (p. 6)

Learning communities are yet another proven national and growing movement aimed to enhance student learning. Over one thousand institutions responded to a survey conducted by the National Resource Center (Tobolowsky, 2008) of which "more than 40% of responding institutions offer learning communities" (p. 98) and some type of experiential learning. Today, given the rise of academic journals, conferences, and organizations devoted to this type of pedagogy and learning, that percent is even higher. According to the National Learning Communities Directory Search, there are currently over 300 institutions that offer learning communities, and 86 of them have started learning communities within the past year. (Washington Center for Improving the Quality of Undergraduate Education)

While these institutions have first-year learning community experiences, many institutions have created more than one type of learning community. Among the many examples, in 1998 Wagner College instituted a campus-wide plan with the focus on "learning by doing"—a curricular approach that centers on the learning-community concept and field or community-based experiential learning. Initially, this consisted of a Freshman Learning Community and as of 2001, the plan consists of three prongs: a freshman (First-Year Freshman Learning Community), an Intermediate (Intermediate Learning Community), and a Senior Learning Community (Senior Learning Community). "LC's are clusters of courses that are linked together by a single theme and that share a common set of students. The faculty plan their LC courses with overlapping assignments, common readings and joint problems so that courses share some common ground" (First-Year Freshman Learning Community).

There are many learning community models. However, please note that unlike reflection, service-learning and civic engagement initiatives which can be associated with merely one course and one instructor, a learning community will require a minimum of two instructors and disciplines. The construction of learning communities mainly takes on five broad forms, and the links created in these models may be created in six broad forms. Therefore, an Institution can first decide on the form of the LC and then choose the link that best meets the needs of the LC.

The five learning community structures can be summarized as follows:

1. "Co-teaching"—
    Usually one course, taught by two instructors, and cross-listed in 2 different disciplines. The students can elect to register for the course in the discipline of choice. This model is found in many institutions.

2. "Linked or cluster courses"—
    From two to four discipline courses, containing the same cohort of students, all sharing a common link/theme; Instructors coordinate their syllabi and assignments so that the classes complement each other. Examples of Institutions include: LaGuardia Community College's Liberal Arts AA Programs, Portland State University's cluster programs, the University of Washington's Interdisciplinary Writing Program; Wagner College's Intermediate and Senior Learning Communities, and Western Michigan University's Honors College Program.

3. "Federated Learning Communities" can take three forms—
    a. Based on a common theme, two separate discipline courses containing the same cohort of students, little or no coordination of syllabi, plus a third course, usually a seminar or skills course, such as writing, or a speech course, where the two disciplines' links are created. The third course is either co-taught, or the class is split up into two groups where each instructor teaches the link(s) between the two disciplines. Among other institutions, at Wagner College, this is found in the Freshman Learning Communities.
    b. "Freshman Interest Groups" within an academic major links three freshmen courses together around a theme with little or no coordination of syllabi. In addition, it includes a peer advising component led by a peer advisor. Examples of institutions include: St. Louis University, Sonoma State University, SUNY at Purchase, the University of Oregon, the University of Missouri, the University of Texas-Arlington, the University of Washington, the University of Wisconsin-Madison, and the University of Wyoming.
    c. Three theme-based courses with little or no coordination of syllabi, in addition to a three-credit seminar taught by a Master Learner (i.e., a professor from a different discipline or faculty tutor) who co-enrolls in all 3 courses and in the seminar, and explores the themes from all 3 courses. Examples of Institutions include:

13

Cabrini College, Indiana University of Pennsylvania, SUNY at Stony Brook, Thomas Nelson Community College, The Community College of Baltimore County, and the University of Texas at Brownsville.

4. "Coordinated Studies" curriculum—
explores a theme or problem rather than discipline methodologies and content; includes multiple teachers from different disciplines-often co-teaching; provides for larger blocks of class time (3-4 hours) and credits (10-15 credits); uses student seminars for exploration of material; requires significant amount of writing; and develops an active collaborative teaching and learning environment. Examples of the institutions that use this type of learning community include: Edmonds Community College, e-Learning at North Seattle Community College, Evergreen State College, Green River Community College, Pacific University Oregon, Seattle Central Community College, Tacoma Community College, and University of British Columbia.

5. "Living-Learning Communities—
A partial or full semester of courses with programs and facilities to support and accommodate a common interest/theme. Among many, some of the institutions that offer this program include: Miami University, Portland State University, St. Lawrence University, Texas A & M, UNC Chapel Hill, University of Arizona, the University of Denver, the University of Illinois at Urbana Champaign, and the University of Iowa; see the National Studies of Living-Learning Programs for more information about living-learning communities (NSLLP).

The "links" that must be created in the above five models of learning communities may be created in the following six ways:
1. *Exploring the same topic(s) or theme(s) of the course from two separate disciplines–*
Example: on the theme of gender discrimination, an economist might discuss its income effect while a sociologist might discuss its social ramifications.
This is most often found in the first learning community model stated above—co-teaching.

2. *Making reference to several specific isolated theory(ies), equation(s), principle(s) in one discipline and how it evolves or is used differently in another discipline–*
Example: the balance sheet in accounting shows that assets must equal liabilities plus owners' equity; however, corporate finance takes the accounting balance sheet and creates a new entry called working capital

requirement which draws upon different accounts from both the assets and liabilities side of the balance sheet. Nonetheless, what is true in both disciplines is that the right side must equal the left side of the balance sheet.

This is most often found in the second learning community model stated above—two courses from two separate disciplines.

3. *The links are not discussed in the 2 classes but referencing may be made on how both disciplines taught in the learning-community can affect a third discipline. This link is the subject of the third class—*
    Example: the disciplines biology and business can be linked to ethics.
    This is most often found in the third learning community model stated above—two courses from two separate disciplines where the link(s) are made in the third course.

4. *Exploring the same topic(s), problem(s), or theme(s) across a series of disciplined courses—*
    Example: the problem of homelessness is discussed in sociology, economics, college writing, and speech courses.
    This is most often found in the fourth learning community model stated above—the coordinated studies curriculum.

5. *Creating isolated outside-the-classroom experience(s) related to some aspect of the linked disciplines—*
    Example: the disciplines economics and religion can have students visiting different neighborhoods while observing the effect religion plays upon the economics of the areas.
    This is found in all the learning community models stated above.

6. *Creating a community-based experience related to some aspect of course(s) in the learning community—*
    Example: this is the case of partnering with local community agencies, either for-profit or not-for-profit organizations, where students are required to devote a certain number of hours working with their assigned local-community partner where the project is related to the learning goals of any course within the learning community.
    This is found in all the learning community models stated above.

Any one of the five learning-community exemplars combined with any of the six links will lead to many permutations of a learning-community model. See Figure 1.1 for a diagrammatic view of these exemplars.

Figure 1.1
Learning Community Models of Linked-Themed Courses
Five Learning-Community Models

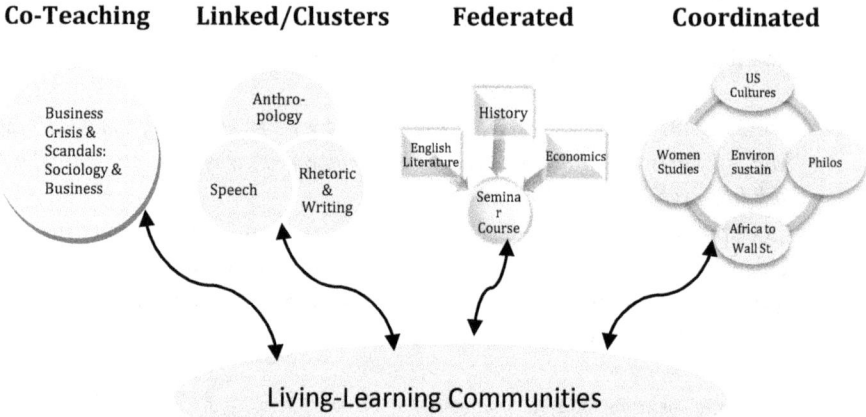

| Co-Teaching | Linked/Clusters | Federated | Coordinated |

Business Crisis & Scandals: Sociology & Business

Anthro-pology

Speech

Rhetoric & Writing

English Literature

History

Economics

Semina r Course

US Cultures

Women Studies

Environ sustain

Philos

Africa to Wall St.

Living-Learning Communities

The Six Links
Exploring the same topic from two separate disciplines
Making reference to a topic in one discipline and how it evolves or is used in another discipline
Referencing may be made on how both disciplines taught in the learning-community can affect a third discipline
Exploring the same topic(s), problem(s), or theme(s) across a series of disciplined courses
Creating an outside-the-classroom experience related to some aspect of the linked disciplines
Creating a community-based experience related to some aspect of the course(s)

Irrespective of form or link, learning communities are effective in bringing about another dimension and increasing awareness and knowledge to discipline-specific learning. While learning communities—forms and links—are not required (as the example of the 3 courses offered in the departmental initiative described in Chapter 4 demonstrates) to offer an effective experiential civic engagement course, experiential learning is often embedded in learning communities, as LCs allow flexibility and have an interdisciplinary focus that brings experiences to life, thus enhancing student learning. As postulated by Bath (2006):

> whilst it continues to be appropriate for universities to be concerned with the quality of their teaching and programs, the interactive, social and collaborative aspects of students' learning experiences, captured in the notion of the Learning Community, are also very important determinants... and so should be included in the focus of attempts at enhancing the quality of student learning. (p. 261)

Especially when the chosen permutation of the learning-community model includes an external partnering component with a local community agency specifically linking the goals of the course(s) to the external experience, this is what is referred to as a service-learning-community, or a civic engagement learning-community (if it also contains an aspect of public concern); or what the Center for Civic Engagement refers to as "citizen scholar." "The objective of the citizen scholar model is to combine academic instruction with implementation of concepts learned in the classroom into the local community." (Citizen Scholar)

PUTTING IT ALL TOGETHER—A COMPREHENSIVE MODEL

Any form of "thought-out" applied learning is preferred to the traditional form of classroom learning. The amount of engagement you wish to add to a course, a departmental or institutional initiative is up to you. Many applied or experiential modalities such as role-playing exercises, field trips, internships, case studies, volunteerism or community service, and service-learning, if constructed properly, will bring to light real-world examples and to some extent enhance a sense of community as well as promote inquiry of broader global and social issues.

While you may partake in one or more of these modalities and it will augment classroom learning, civic engagement models go beyond the above-cited experiences, and show how these engaged learning modalities serve to:

- put into practice what the students are learning in the classroom;
- witness the imperfections and incompleteness of the models and frameworks read in textbooks;
- deepen student engagement of civic/public issues;
- extend the College's connection to the community and strengthen its civic engagement mission;
- highlight students' positive exposure in the media reinforcing critical, civic and public speaking skills;

17

- foster a campus environment where students, faculty, administrators, alumni and community members are actively engaged; and
- allow instructors the opportunity to develop interactive teaching practices, knowledge and research agenda.

Furthermore, if we combine civic engagement with reflection and if the course we are planning on teaching is offered as part of a learning community, the experiences to and from all participants, are enhanced.

The construction, considerations and implementation of this type of model is discussed fully in Chapter 3—an experiential civic learning model. Additionally, the construct of this model can be included as part of a departmental civic learning initiative as shown in Chapter 4. But, before exploring the considerations and construction of these models, a note on funding and grants is in order—the focus of Chapter 2.

Chapter 2

Project Funding & Grants

This Chapter Contains:

IS FUNDING NEEDED?
  The Budget
PROCESS FOR OBTAINING FUNDING
  Funding Proposals (Established Grants, Internal Funding, & New Grants)
SOURCES FOR GRANT OPPORTUNITIES

IS FUNDING NEEDED?

As with any project undertaken in real life, after the conception stage, and before the construction stage begins, we should first evaluate the need for funding—will a budget be wanted and/or needed to carry out the initiative? In this process, consider the following three steps.

Step I, ask yourself, do you need a budget for your experiential initiative? If the answer is no, please note that you do not need funding in order to design a successful experiential course. In fact, while many of these initiatives start with a small faculty support budget, mainly to compensate the faculty for the "extra" work required in developing a service-learning, civic engagement, learning communities and/or reflective practices' course, after the development stage, most initiatives are sustained without or with a minimal budget. As suggested by Inspired to Serve, service-learning efforts may begin with volunteer leaders who are passionate about the vision, but at some point, you will need some funding to accomplish your goals. "This may be as simple as funding to purchase supplies for a project or [on a much broader scale] ongoing financial support to staff and to coordinate the network." (Inspired to Serve)

If, on the other hand, the answer to the above question is yes, you will need to decide how much money will be required or desired.

Step II, how much money would you need to successfully carry out your experiential project and what can you spend it on?

The Budget

In order for you to construct a budget and arrive at a desired funding amount, you could incorporate the costs of all materials needed to design and carry out your newly constructed experiential engagement course commensurate with the goals of the course and the activities that will be required to reach those goals. These material items can include, and should not be limited to, the purchase of: computer memory sticks, a video camera, a projector with screen, printing costs associated with brochures or posters, gift items (i.e., pens or pads with logo) for the community recipients, meeting/seminar/conference refresh-ments, travel for you and/or students to and from the placement, and varied office supplies.

Additionally, you may include your stipend and the expenses associated with your scholarly pursuits directly linked to this project. Please note that not all funding agents will allow you to budget a stipend; however, most will allow you to include budgetary expenses associated with scholarly activities. Scholarly activities can take many forms, and it is up to you to justify why you are seeking funding for these activities.

Again, please note that not all funding agents will allow you to budget expenses associated with a conference, unless your work has undergone a review process. This may mean that you can budget the associated expenses only if: a) your paper has been accepted for presentation, b) you have been asked by the organizers of the conference to present, c) you are organizing a session, d) you are on a panel or are a discussant, or e) you are doing a poster presentation—all associated with the experiential initiative. Expense items for the conference can include: conference registration fees, all travel costs (e.g., plane, train, car service, and/or miles and tolls if taking your own car) to and from the conference, parking, hotel, tips, and daily meal allowance for the period you are at the conference.

Lastly, Step III, if funding is required or desired, you will need to seek sources for your funding needs.

So, where can you obtain funding?

PROCESS FOR OBTAINING FUNDING

There are three main sources for obtaining funding—two external and one internal.

Source I: partaking in an established institutional grant with monies received from outside your institution's sources.

Source II: asking your Administration for funding (internal-institutional funding).

Source III: writing a grant proposal and seeking external grant funding, preferably with the help of a grant coordinator or your Institutional Advancement Office.

Figure 2.1 can provide a snapshot for the above three sources.

Figure 2.1.
Flow Chart for Seeking Funding

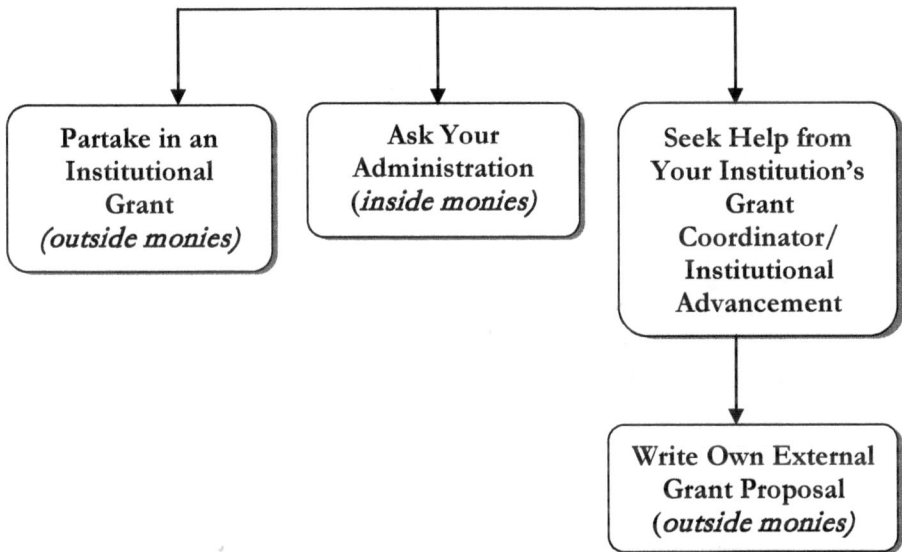

The Established Grant

Source I: If your institution offers you the opportunity to be part of an external grant, you should seize the opportunity. Most of the time, even if you were not on the ground-floor in the writing of the external grant, you will still be able to work within the grant's parameters. While this may not be optimal as earmarked line items may not be in your desired amount (e.g., you would have wanted $1,000 for the printing of brochures, but the grant only allows for $500) or, desired budgeted line items may have been omitted (e.g., you would have liked to receive a stipend of $1,000 for all your extra efforts associated with this endeavor, but the grant does not include this line item) you can still reap some of the benefits (i.e., ready money) for portions of your endeavor, and it makes your case stronger if you also decide to seek an outside funder (i.e., most funders like the fact that your project has merit and has previously received approval.) However, if you received prior funding and you are ready to submit an updated proposal for external funding, please make sure your new proposal explains how the previous project has informed your new proposed initiative. Funding agencies like to see how you have learned and progressed from prior projects.

The Internal Funding Proposal

Source II: If your institution does not offer you the opportunity to be part of an existing grant, you could request internal funding for all or part of your projected budget from your Administration (i.e., your department Chair, Dean, Institutional Advancement/grant office, or Provost), or request funding as part of your institution's faculty aid budget (if it exists). In reaching out to the Administration or completing your application for faculty aid, in order to increase your chances of receiving the funds, it is recommended that you write a formal grant proposal and supply the following information:

- The goals of your course and how they closely align with the goals of your department and the institution;
- community partner(s) information and their goals;
- students' projected deliverables;
- timeline for project (e.g., one semester initiative or span over two consecutive semesters); and,
- a detailed budget.

If you are seeking funds from your Institution and your budget is rather large and/or your project spans over multiple semesters, you may want to consider submitting two proposed budgets—one budget per semester; or a "minimal" budget (i.e., what you "really need") plus an "expanded" budget (i.e., what you "would like to receive") to complete your project. This will enhance the probability of receiving at least partial monies.

The New Grant Proposal

Source III: If you need funding and your institution does not have funds to support your endeavors, you can seek funding from outside your institution. This would naturally entail you finding a donor and writing and submitting a formal grant proposal. However, before undertaking such a task, it is recommended that you first seek help. Guidance can be obtained from the grant coordinator at your Institution or from your Institutional Advancement Office. Most schools have a grant coordinator, whether it is a full-time staff person (sometimes also found in your Institutional Advancement Office) or an instructor with added responsibilities. Even if the grant coordinator or your Institutional Advancement Office cannot find a donor for your project, they will be able to review your proposal and make suggestions—especially with respect to your budget. Additionally, you may want to seek advice from colleagues at other institutions that have successfully received grants on similar projects. They may be able to share with you their budgets, how they wrote the proposals, and other helpful insights.

Lastly, if you need funding, your Institution does not have funds to support your initiative; your Institution does not have a grant coordinator nor an Institutional Advancement Office; the grant coordinator and the Institutional Advancement Office do not have a database in which to search for possible donors for your project; or guidance from a colleague from another institution is not an option; this should not discourage you from writing and submitting a proposal for funding. So where can you start? With the plethora of publications, seminars, conferences, and work being conducted in some form of experiential learning, many grant opportunities exist in this field of scholarly research.

SOURCES FOR GRANT OPPORTUNITIES

Unless you have access to private donors, places where you can reach out to fund your initiative(s) are: your city and state political offices, federally-funded programs, and private organizational donors.

With respect to your local and state political offices, in order to increase the odds of being awarded funding, you may want to consider the following: write your grant proposal and send them a cover letter stating how this project will help build their constituency base; how the goals of your initiative match the goals of their campaign; and how the project is timely and is essential for the neighborhood or the well-being of the residents. You may wish to invite them to come and speak or address the class and/or community; and/or if you feel comfortable, invite them to give input in the shaping of your initiative. Naturally, the above guidelines serve as suggestions and do not guarantee you will be successful in obtaining funding.

With respect to federally-funded programs, the guidelines, timelines, forms that will need to be completed and all other information that you will need to supply to qualify for funding are specified and different for each program. These programs and their guidelines can be found by searching the U.S. Department of Education (link included in Figure 2.2.). As federally-funded programs change according to economic times, you should check the website periodically.

Figure 2.2.
Funding Organizations/Search Engines

Name of Organization	Website Address
Bill & Melinda Gates Foundation	http://www.gatesfoundation.org/grantseeker/Pages/
Campus Compact	http://www.compact.org/category/events-jobs-grants- more/grants-and-fellowships/
David & Lucile Packard Foundation	http://www.packard.org/grants
Ford Foundation	http://www.fordfoundation.org/Grants
Learn & Serve America	http://www.learnandserve.gov/for_organizations/funding/index.asp
National Science Foundation	http://www.nsf.gov/funding/
Project Pericles	http://www.projectpericles.org/projectpericles/programs/ classroom/cec/
Teagle Foundation	http://www.teaglefoundation.org/grantmaking/overview.aspx
The Foundation Center	http://foundationcenter.org
U.S. Department of Education	http://www.ed.gov
U.S. Small Business Administration	http://www.sba.gov/content/facts-about-government-grants
W. K. Kellogg Foundation	http://www.wkkf.org/grants/grants-database.aspx

With respect to organizational donors, as a ready-reference, Figure 2.2 lists two funding search engines and ten organizations with their corresponding WebPages that fund service-learning, civic engagement, learning community, and reflective practice endeavors.

Grants from the organizations listed in figure 2.2 are usually awarded to educators, community-based organizations, and service-learning/civic engagement coordinators to fund service-learning/civic engagement projects or programs. Some will require a mini-grant orientation session, training and/or periodic reporting, but all will require some type of evaluation report upon the completion of the project or program. Do not ignore this last step as you may not receive full funding, or you will be ineligible to receive funding in the future.

Nonetheless, while funding for your civic engagement course would be a "nice to have" even if you do not have an allotted budget, with careful planning, and maybe with minor modifications to your project, you can still construct a successful experiential course.

With the basic questions and resources of funding addressed, we can turn our attention to Chapter 3, our next chapter, for the construction, considerations, and challenges associated with a civic engagement course, with community partners stemming from a learning community, and with using reflective practices.

Chapter 3

An Experiential Civic Learning Model

This Chapter Contains:

Chapter 1 emphasized the fact that students' learning is best achieved when instructors incorporate an experiential component to their course and when students can come to the realization that what they are learning goes beyond the specific discipline/topics that are being taught in a particular course; that is, classroom learning should not exist in a vacuum. The benefits of incorporating an experiential civic engagement component to a course cannot be ignored. As such, as posed previously, this field of pedagogy has seen tremendous growth in interest and has spurred conferences, journals, and funding opportunities in the U.S. and abroad.

This chapter delves into the development of an experiential civic engagement model emanating within a learning community. Discussed are: the challenges and considerations in the construction of a community-based civic engagement course; the importance of a mutual support system; changes in pedagogy and epistemology; integrating civic engagement in a traditional course; and offers two examples of the experiential civic learning model—from considerations in the selection and changes that must be made to traditionally-delivered courses and curriculum as well as partnership(s), project, and student and faculty deliverables—one initiative emanating from an Institutional grant, and another from an Instructor-written grant. In addition, as a resource tool, this chapter offers a "To-Do" checklist of activities that are recommended to take place before, during, and after the course ends. This chapter ends with the top seven lessons learned from educators undertaking these initiatives.

CHALLENGES & CONSTRUCTION OF A COMMUNITY-BASED CIVIC ENGAGEMENT COURSE

In the construction of a community-based civic engagement course, irrespective of the discipline and level, all courses with an experiential component face four major challenges:

1. the need for a mutual support system—agreement and cooperation by all participants;

2. changes that must be made in pedagogy and epistemology;

3. integrating the civic engagement component to the course; and,

4. assessing the "value-added" of offering this type of experiential course.

Challenge 1: Mutual Support System

In addressing the first challenge, mutual support at all levels is vital. But cooperation, agreement, and support must be a two-way street. From the institution's perspective, the faculty member of the civic engagement course should have the support of his/her department and support of his/her institution's administration. This will enable the Instructor to more easily secure space on campus for meetings or public venues, printing and postage privileges, and office supplies, and the campus' public relations person to write and place a promotional piece of prose on the partnership and project, or any other item or service required to carry out the initiative.

Similarly, the community partner's local site supervisor(s) or the people who will be integrally involved in the students' education should also obtain their administration's support. This will enable them to make quicker decisions and share in some or all of the material and support structures needed to carry out the project.

Additionally, the Instructor of the course and the Site Supervisor must cooperate and support the learning needs of the students. This is a crucial step. As the Instructor is no longer the sole educator of the course, if the Instructor and the Site Supervisor are not in total accord as to all of the goals and phases of the project, the students will receive mixed messages and their learning and satisfaction with the experience will be less than optimal.

Lastly, the students will need to cooperate with and support the community partner as well as the instructor of the course. Students will need to be told either during class sessions, written on the syllabus, posted on course's website, or in all or other venues, the roles of all participants in the initiative and be given clear expectations and demarcation of boundaries. Figure 1 demonstrates such a structure. The "experience" will be heightened with open communication, cooperation, agreement, and support at all levels.

Figure 3.1.
Mutual Support Structure

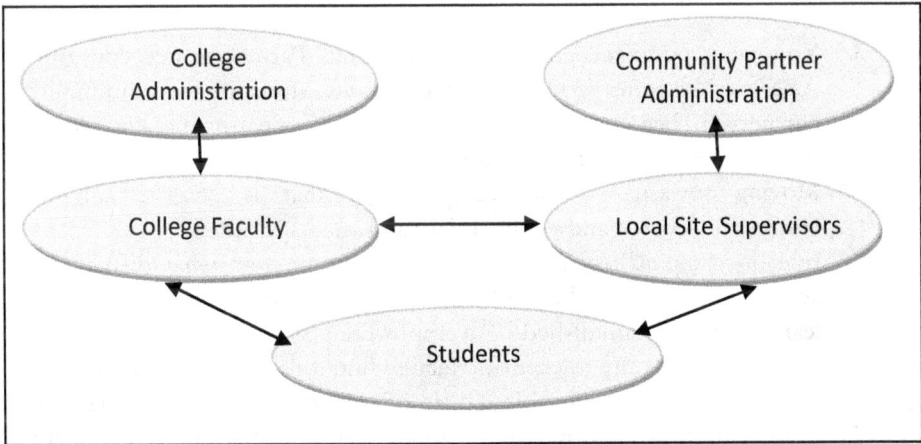

Challenge 2: Changes in Pedagogy and Epistemology

You should not teach an experiential learning course as a traditional, in-the-classroom course. Pedagogical and epistemological changes, the second challenge cited above in the construction of a civic engagement course, will need to be made and can be reflected in the following three ways:

1. The syllabus is the students' first exposure to the goals and expectations of the course. Therefore, it is important that your syllabus reflect the civic and experiential nature of your course. While it is not possible to incorporate all nuances of the out-of-classroom experience into the syllabus, the more details you incorporate in the document, the more issues and concerns you will avoid, and the less you will experience miscommunications, false expectations, and student complaints.

2. You will need to allocate time for a discussion of the civic engagement project, student comments and feedback, and overall reflection of the experience. You can devote a portion of class time or choose some type of online discussion boards for these activities. If you choose to have reflection in an online setting, you should monitor that students are "actively" posting their reflections and that their concerns are being addressed. As a barometer for the average class time devoted to experiential activities, NSSE 2010 data report the following: 3% of class time was devoted to experiential activities in English courses; 6% in Business courses; 9% in Psychology courses; and 25% in Biology courses. (National Survey of Student Engagement)

3. You will need to recognize your Community Partner as a co-educator. As argued by Jones (2003), "allowing faculty, students, and community partners to become part of the process of constructing knowledge requires shifting from a culture of argument to one of dialogue. Moving toward a reflective pedagogy that is student-centered, community-based, and experiential fundamentally redefines the faculty role on campus." (p. 2) This concept may be somewhat difficult to accept at first, but, if this is not realized, your students' experiences and learning will be diminished. "As empowering as service-learning can be in redefining faculty roles, many faculty find it difficult to relinquish the comfortable and predictable nature of classroom work, particularly at the beginning of the process." (Jones, 2003, p. 2) Additionally, your students will need to view their community partner(s) as co-educators in order for them to put forth the same type of effort in the field as in the classroom. This may be reinforced with having your community partner be part of the students' grading process.

Challenge 3: Integrating Civic Engagement

With respect to the third challenge, integrating the civic engagement component into the course, the following examples (the first example from an institutional grant and the second from a faculty-written grant) show how an established course within a learning-community was altered to incorporate a civic engagement component and community partners to deepen student learning, students' perception of learning, reflective practices, oral and written communication skills, and to render assistance to the community partner, build a better relationship between the institution and community partner, and bring awareness of the needs of the community to the students, school, and the community at large.

CIVIC ENGAGEMENT COURSE CONSTRUCTION #1 - FROM AN INSTITUTIONAL GRANT

The following shows the construction of a civic engagement course within a learning-community emanating from an institutional grant. From Chapter 1, the learning community model employed was #2—two courses with two instructors—and the link employed was #6— creating a community-based experience related to some aspect of the course(s) in the learning community.

Wagner College was chosen as one of seven schools (the other 6 schools were: The Richard Stockton College of New Jersey, St. Lawrence University, University of Massachusetts Boston, University of Michigan, University of South Dakota, Virginia Wesleyan College) out of one-hundred-thirty-seven applicants for a grant from the Center for Liberal Education and Civic Engagement, to assess and deepen the pedagogies and practices of civic engagement and campus-community partnerships. The grant, *Journey toward Democracy: Power, Voice and the Public Good*, a national dialogue project, combined democratic pedagogy and dialogues amongst multiple stakeholders—an inter-institutional team of faculty, students, and staff—to strengthen the under-graduate experience, the campus community, and the civic mission of the college.

In the second year of the grant's inception, the Department of Business Administration decided to partake in this initiative. However, the willingness to "join" was not an automatic process. As discussed in Chapter 2, while the Department was fortunate that an institutional grant with funding from an outside source was made available to all departments on campus that wanted to join this initiative, guidelines had to be met, and a competitive process had been set in place. Accordingly, the Department wrote a report on how it would meet the guidelines set forth in the grant and a detailed grant proposal along with the report was submitted for evaluation. Therefore, for the academic year 2003-04, the Department of Business Administration joined the Departments of Nursing, Government & Politics, Education, History, and Sociology, to further the mission to deliver a civic engagement course, deepen student reflection and strengthen campus-community partnerships.

31

With the matter of funding established, the choice of a course and partner(s) had to be decided.

Course Selection

In selecting a course for this grant, the Department chose the Senior Reflective Tutorial (RFT) course, one of the linked-courses in the Senior Learning Community (SLC), to be part of this initiative. The ultimate goal of the Senior Program is that all Business seniors merge the breadth of a liberal education with the depth of specialized knowledge into a real-world applied practice. The traditional SLC is comprised of a senior capstone course; Business Policy & Strategy, which focuses on the development of analytical as well as professional skills by engaging students in rigorous teamwork computer-simulated studies; and the RFT. This arrangement allows the students to synthesize various elements of the strategic process into a well-formulated plan that addresses all aspects of a company's internal and external environments. The themes discussed in the capstone course are not only applied to the experiential component—a 100-hour practicum in the student's chosen concentration of study—but are also discussed during the RFT class sessions. Included in the RFT course's discussions are issues pertaining to all aspects of professional development, with emphasis on the challenges of the transition from being a student to a civic-minded professional. The purpose of these rigorous team-oriented learning community classes is to prepare students for their chosen career or entrance to graduate school. (Business Administration Senior Program)

While other courses could have been chosen for this initiative, it is in the Instructor's best interest to choose classes that are either a "special topic" course rather than a required course in the major, or a required course that offers multiple sections in the same semester. Students should be given the ability to self-select and not feel forced to register and participate in an experiential civic engagement course; otherwise, you may meet resistance. Therefore, because of the RFT's fit (i.e., it was part of a learning community and already had an experiential component, albeit an internship) it seemed "natural" that this course be chosen as the civic engagement course to be part of this grant.

Partnership(s) Selection

Similar to the quest for choosing a course, the quest for a community partner or partners needed careful consideration.

As a general guideline in your search for a community partner, you may first want to explore the following five considerations: the institutional goals of your community partner's organization, their interest in partnering, their availability to work with you and your students, location and accommodations, and the project.

First, the goals of your community partner's organization must match the goals of your Institution, department, and course in some aspect. As an example, if your favorite organization is Special Olympics and you want to use them as your community partner because the mission of Special Olympics is to provide year-round sports training and athletic competition, you may find resistance if you want your students to develop a financial literacy program for the Special Olympics participants. However, this organization may well fit with a course devoted to marketing events.

Second, your community partner should show an active interest and enthusiasm in partnering with your institution, your class, and with you. As stated previously, your community partner should be your students' co-educator in this initiative. Therefore, if you sense resistance, a lack of cooperation, or ambivalence toward the project or partnership, you may want to consider finding another community partner.

Third, the ideal situation would be if the community organization would assign a dedicated person for this collaboration. While you should guide your students in their experiential initiative, if your community partner is willing to devote time to the experiential project, be readily available to work with your students directly as well as answer questions and offer suggestions, you will avoid miscommunications, and the expectations for the project's deliverable(s) will be met.

Fourth, you should consider the location and accommodations of the organization. Are they located close to the College where students can easily go and meet with them? If not, does your Institution provide transportation? Do the students have cars or is public transportation readily available? If the students will be conducting their work at the site, does the organization have the space capacity to house the students at their location? If not, can you or your Institution provide the space? Is there special equipment that is needed? If so, will the organization provide it, or will your Institution be able to provide it? These types of questions will need to be addressed before the course and partnership can begin and develop.

Fifth, full agreement is vital for all aspects of the students' outside-the-classroom learning experience. This includes and is not limited to: days and hours spent in the community, reporting structure, type of experience, and deliverables. The more you can agree upon and solidify the details, preferably before the start of the semester, the higher your success rate for the experiential initiative. If you are not able to come to terms with your community partner on these items, you should continue searching for another community partner.

Echoing the above, as voiced by other practitioners, good partnerships are founded on good communication, respect, mutual benefit, and governance structures that allow democratic decision-making, process improvement, and resource sharing (Benson & Harkavy, 2001; Campus Compact, 2000; CCPH, 1999; Mihalynuk & Seifer, 2002; Schumaker, Reed, & Woods, 2000; Worrall, 2007).

The search for a community partner for the civic engagement 2003-04 initiative led to the Staten Island Economic Development Center (SIEDC). Prior to the beginning of the semester, a preliminary meeting was called to allow each participant to understand the needs and explore how each could contribute to the initiative's mission, while also meeting the goals of the respective organizations, the course, and the students. At the conclusion of this first meeting, the idea for a project arose. A subsequent meeting was set up to further explore the scope of the project, identify goals, etc.

Adjustments to Curriculum

In complying with the civic engagement grant by offering a course devoted to civic engagement and community partnerships, the Business Department made four adjustments to its institutionalized traditional RFT course. (Service-Learning Ideas and Curricular Examples)

First, traditionally, the Institution's business students were allowed to complete a field placement of their choosing, according to their interest or field of specialization. With the RFT devoted to civic engagement, the students were not allowed to do a practicum of their choice but instead, they were partnered with SIEDC. In addition, the students were required to maintain a log/diary of their field work that, at a minimum, included the dates they attended the site, a brief description of the duties performed on each date, and the signature of an appropriate community supervisory person verifying the dates and quality of work performed. This component, the completed 100-hours of the practicum with their community partner, constituted 30% of the students' final grade for the RFT course.

Second, the students in the traditional RFT course were allowed to choose a research topic of their own selection for their comprehensive end-of-semester academic research paper. However, for the RFT devoted to service-learning, the required senior thesis project was a civic needs-assessment plan of the area, involving applied and research-based learning. The expectation was of a well-defined and rigorous document that would ideally encapsulate the students' field experiences, research, and personal observations, integrating them into a larger academic theme and body of literature. This component, the senior thesis, constituted 50% of the students' final grade for the RFT course.

Third, the weekly RFT meetings included class discussion of assigned readings; class discussion of students' field experiences and progress on their senior theses; a discussion of professional, career, and civic development issues through guest speaker presentations; field trips; and other suitable on/off campus events. This third component of the course did not differ drastically from the traditional RFT except that the guest lecturers discussed their research and best practices with field-based projects. Participation of these specialized events completed the remaining 20% of the students' final grades.

Lastly, the traditional RFT did not have a presentation component while the RFT devoted to civic engagement required the students to present at multiple venues. A copy of the abstract of the Civic Engagement Senior Reflective Tutorial Course Syllabus, discussed above, is posted on the National Service-Learning Clearinghouse, SLiCE database; and the Civic Engagement Senior Reflective Tutorial Course Syllabus is posted on Campus Compact's website: <http://www.compact.org/syllabi/senior-capstone/business-administration-department-senior-reflective-tutorial/4186/>. You should feel free to search the Campus Compact database for other civic engagement/service-learning syllabi from many varied disciplines at many institutions.

Once the course, the community partner, the potential project, and syllabus are identified and formalized, in order to avoid student confusion in registering for a traditional versus a civic-engagement course, for registration purposes, some type of notation is suggested to be placed next to the civic engagement course's name or number. As an example, an asterisk can be placed next to the course's number (e.g., BU400*) with a note stating that it was a civic engagement course. As the students who enroll in the course devoted to civic engagement are self-selective, very little resistance will be met with the experiential component of the course and the pedagogical adjustments that are made to allow for this type of learning.

"The Project" — Student & Faculty Project Deliverables

In continuing with the above example in constructing a civic engagement course, after the start of the semester, the six business students enrolled in the

RFT, the instructor, and the community members from SIEDC sat for a third meeting to solidify the project—to identify the issues surrounding the St. George area and arrive at a concrete action plan. Thus, from the beginning of February through the end of April of the spring semester, the six business students, operating as business consultants, tried to accomplish their goal of identifying the economic, social, and civic problematic issues of the St. George area of Staten Island. Collaboratively, they wrote an eighteen-question open-ended questionnaire and personally interviewed over sixty members of the community, including local public officials; government leaders; workers; property and business owners; schools' administrators, staff and students; and residents of the area. The culmination of their efforts, the St. George Action Plan, reflected the needs and wants of the St. George community, and offered solutions to the issues that many believed have to this day hindered the development of the area. The final needs-assessment plan (bound copies of which were distributed to all members of the community and available at the Institution's library) not only identified ten key concerns of the area, but also included short and long-term solutions, as well as identified local agencies with responsibilities for the implementation of each revitalization component.

In addition to the research, the students were exposed to making public appearances. They held a press conference (Students, 2004) and made two formal presentations of their findings. (St. George Action Plan-A Civic Engagement Endeavor, 2004) and (St. George Action Plan-A Civic Engagement Endeavor Symposium, 2004)

Public, written exposure on this initiative arose from four local newspaper articles in the *Staten Island Advance* (SIEDC to Announce St. George project with Wagner College, 2004), (Wagner College Student Stephanie Bower Speaks about the St. George Action Plan, 2004), (Island Business Leaders Keep the Economy Moving, 2004) and, (Wagner College Business Team Up to Improve St. George, 2004).

Furthermore, as a testament of how this field of study can and has expanded into a faculty member's research publication agenda, the instructor of the course was accepted to present at a conference (Lo Re, 2004) and published a peer-reviewed journal article devoted to this initiative (Lo Re, St. George Action Plan-A Civic Engagement Endeavor, 2004).

CIVIC ENGAGEMENT COURSE CONSTRUCTION #2—FROM AN INSTRUCTOR-WRITTEN GRANT

The following shows the construction of a civic engagement course within a learning-community emanating from a grant written by the instructor of the course. As a result of the success of the spring 2004 semester's civic engagement undertaking, during the subsequent academic year, in an effort to bring the same type of experience to the new cohort of Business Administration undergraduate seniors, the Department wanted to offer another civic engagement course. Therefore, the Senior Reflective Tutorial housed in the Senior Learning Community was de-facto established as the grant's participatory course. However, the community partner and the funding considerations needed to be revisited.

Funding and Partnership Selection Revisited

With respect to funding, the Institutional prior year's grant funding had ended. The Department worked with the Institution's grant coordinator and Institutional Advancement Office to identify a donor. This search led to the U.S Department of Small Business Services (see website listing in Chapter 2, Figure 2.2). In searching the database, a $10,000 grant provided by the Honorable Michael McMahon, Council Member, through the NYC Department of Small Business Services Neighborhood Development to work on commercial revitalization programs in neighboring communities was available and fit the goals of the identified civic engagement course. However, before the grant proposal could be written, submitted, and hopefully awarded, the project and the community partner or partners first had to be identified.

The Department's first proclivity in choosing a partner was to once again contact SIEDC. However, SIEDC did not have another project of the same magnitude, they were in the midst of changing personnel, and the Department was eager to expand the Institution's cohort of community partners. Therefore, a new partner was warranted.

Staten Island, New York (where Wagner College is located), has three main local development not-for-profit organizations. Thus the Department approached them with this initiative's proposal and forged partnerships with the Downtown Staten Island Council, the Northfield, and the West Brighton Local Development Corporations (LDCs). Similar to the working relationship with SIEDC, many meetings and discussions ensued with these new partners.

While the goals of the Institution, the Department, and the basic goals of the course, as well as the changes in pedagogy would remain the same as with the prior year's initiative, a change in the community partner (from one partner to three partners), the scope of the project, and corresponding student deliverables had to be revisited.

Project and Deliverables Revisited

Upon the awarding of this grant, the course was established. That year, nine seniors enrolled in the civic engagement RFT course. These students were divided (according to their preferences and skill sets) into three cohorts—a team of three students per LDC—to devote their services toward furthering the commercial revitalization programs within their LDC's respective geographic areas.

Collectively, the students prepared a brochure for the press conference (Wagner College Students to Intern With Local Development Groups, 2005). At the completion of the semester, the students presented their accomplishments to the Staten Island and Wagner College communities (College Seniors Give Reports on Local Involvement, 2005). The collaborative efforts with the Downtown Staten Island Council, the Northfield Community, and the West Brighton LDCs produced the extensive deliverables noted in Figure 3.2.

Additionally, the course's civic engagement efforts and notice of the students' final presentation was featured in *The Periclean Progress* E-Newsletter. (Wagner College-Notable Program Activities:Campus, Classroom, and Community, 2005)

The above two exemplars delved into the process and addressed the first three challenges in constructing a community-based civic engagement course. The last challenge, assessing the value-added of offering this type of experiential course follows.

Challenge 4: Assessing "Value Added"

The fourth challenge that must be confronted for the construction of a course devoted to civic engagement is assessing the "value-added" of offering this type of experiential course. This challenge, due to its length and depth, is deserving of much attention and is discussed in two chapters—Chapters 5 and 6— Indirect and Direct Assessment, respectively.

However, before concluding this chapter, in order to bring the construction of the experiential learning model full circle, a "to do" task checklist and lessons learned in the development of experiential courses are discussed next.

The "To-Do" Checklist: Before, During & After

While the descriptions above should have given you a good glimpse of some of the challenges and construction considerations in developing a civic engagement course within a learning community with internal and external grant funding, what are the actual "to do's" of such a course? You will undoubtedly need to set aside some time before, during and after the semester ends for successfully carrying through your civic engagement endeavor. Figure 3.3 offers a checklist of the "to do's" or tasks broken down by time period for the semester —before the semester begins, during the semester, and after the semester ends. It is meant to be used as a relatively complete reminder of the tasks and activities you may wish to complete throughout your initiative.

Upon inspection of the "to do" checklist, you should note that there are 18 items that should be considered and/or completed before the semester begins and 7 items each that should be completed during and after the semester ends; thus the majority of an Instructor's work and time is spent before the semester begins.

LESSONS LEARNED

To conclude, in constructing and offering civic engagement courses, educators espouse the following seven lessons learned:

- Having a grant is a plus but not a must.
- Support at all levels is critical to the success of the program.
- You should consider your community partner as your co-educator.
- Changes in pedagogy, and to some degree, epistemology, are inevitable.
- Allow for additional preparation time for classes.
- Prepare your assessment tools early.
- A well designed and implemented program can be mutually rewarding for students, faculty, the community partner(s), and the university.

Figure 3.2.
Students' Civic Engagement Course
Deliverables at Staten Island's LDCs

Downtown S.I. LDC	Northfield LDC	West Brighton LDC
• Promoted the waterfront community by providing a quarterly newsletter and instituting a graffiti removal and control program. • Researched and identified foundation, bank, corporation, and government grants that would be applicable for the Downtown Staten Island Council. • Reviewed and updated statistical information that included the types of businesses in the area, number of existing shops, and vacant storefront reports. • Created relationships between local merchants and the art community to provide exposure for artists while enhancing the business district.	• Multi-tasked organizational, developmental and outreach duties, including property research at Borough Hall, inventoried current property conditions & usage within the catchment area, and consistently provided outreach to educate the merchants &property owners. • Business Improvement District (BID) planning--creating a database of all properties with all pertinent information as required by the NYC Department of Small Business Services. Responsible for education and outreach to the business community regarding the BID process. • Event planning--coordinating all aspects of Northfield's community events. Responsible for site selection program, flyer designs, coordinating with other agencies, mailing, phones, and follow-ups. • Feasibility study of NASCAR.	• ShopABLE NYC Program-a matching funds program to entice merchants to make their shops or restaurants "Americans with Disabilities Act" compliant. Through interpersonal collaborations, research & marketing, they created brochures and showed the benefits of what the program has to offer to the S.I. community. • Kickoff Event introducing a menu in Braille for disabled people in the community. • Storefront Renovation Project. • BOC Women's Business Center marketing and promotion. Collected and analyzed data to measure past year's performance & put together a marketing plan focusing on growth for struggling businesses on Staten Island. • The Arts & Crafts Show and Sale in St. George is an annual event on which all three LDCs collaborated. They prepared marketing & logistical assistance for this event.

Figure 3.3.
The "To-Do" Check List

Before Course Begins
____ Seek funding (optional)

____ Identify the civic engagement courses

____ Identify the community partner

____ Meet with college's administration for approval of partnership/project

____ Identify the community partner's key contacts

____ Identify community partner's needs

____ Agree on the actual project(s) students will undertake

____ Identify who will monitor the students while at the placement

____ Discuss & identify student screening(s) before they can undertake work (e.g., blood/urine test, background checks)—if applicable

____ Establish & agree on a grading system with community partner

____ Develop syllabus

____ Develop assessment tool(s)

____ Develop student evaluation forms for community partner

____ Establish timeline (i.e., when students will start/end, deliverables, evaluations ...)

____ Ensure community partner has received approval of this partnership from their administration

____ Establish how will problems be communicated

____ Advertise course

____ Recruit and advise students

During Semester
____ Administer assessment tool(s)—pre if appropriate

____ Allow time for reflection in the classroom

____ Follow up with students on their progress

____ Follow up with community partner

____ Review of final product produced by students

____ Decide on how the final product will be presented to the community partner and/or school's administration

____ Administer assessment tool(s)—post if appropriate

After Semester Ends
____ Send final product to community partner

____ Send thank-you note to community partner

____ Discuss what went right/wrong during the semester with your community partner

____ Analyze assessment tool(s)

____ Schedule follow-up date to discuss next semester's collaboration

____ Make changes/adjustments based upon discussion with community partner & assessment tools for next semester

____ Report results to college administration

Chapter 4

Departmental Civic Engagement Model

This Chapter Contains:

CONSIDERATIONS IN CREATING A DEPARTMENTAL MODEL
Selection & Number of Courses, Number of Hours
Single vs. Multiple Community Partner Considerations
Student-Community Goals, Project, Experiences
DEPARTMENTAL MODEL EXEMPLAR: A SINGLE COMMUNITY PARTNER
UTILIZING SEQUENCED & DIFFERENT-FIELD COURSES
ADVANTAGES TO FACULTY

In Chapter 3, a single course's civic engagement model with a community partner and partners was proposed. In putting together a departmental experiential civic initiative, we should look to build upon single civic engagement courses with respect to civic engagement efforts commensurate with students' levels of academic competence. However, in creating a departmental initiative, Jones (2003) asks us to consider "how to move the fragmented and insular work of the academy toward greater connection and agency." This will require faculty (as well as administrators) to examine strategies for "shifting from a culture of privatized work to one of collective work, both within the department and across the institution." It will also require "connecting professional expertise to public discourse for wider civic engagement and as a way of approaching the construction of knowledge."(p. 1)

This chapter discusses the considerations needed to construct a departmental civic engagement initiative that can be applied to any department. These considerations include: selection of courses, number of involved courses, student experiential hours, number of partnerships, student-community goals, project, and types of experiences. As an addition to the individual course exemplars in the previous chapter, this chapter highlights the Department of Business Administration's model in delivering experiential service and civic engagement courses. The chapter concludes with the advantages to the faculty in creating such an endeavor.

CONSIDERATIONS IN CREATING A DEPARTMENTAL MODEL

If we combine the elements of Chapter 3 and incorporate the decision to utilize a single or multiple community partners, the courses, project, and assessment plan—and keep in mind open communications, collaborations and approvals at all levels and among all participants—a departmental civic experiential initiative can prove to be a successful and rewarding experience for all participants.

To build a cohesive departmental program where each course complements and builds upon the other and where there is assessment of not only each course but also of the departmental initiative, it is vital that the instructors of the participating courses consider the following: selection and number of courses that will be part of this departmental initiative, the student hours to be devoted to the experience, the choice of a single or multiple community partners, the experiential project, goals, and the activities which will also be used for assessment.

Selection & Number of Courses, Number of Hours

In deciding the selection of courses, the number of courses that can and should be part of the departmental initiative and the number of hours the students will devote to the experiential portion of each course; the general goals of the department are what should guide all of these decisions. Each department has established goals that permeate throughout all courses (e.g., increased proficiency in subject-matter, writing, speaking, critical thinking, etc.). Reference should be made to these goals in establishing the guidelines of this departmental initiative while asking: What are the specific goals of the department in delivering experiential learning? And then proceeding to ask questions such as: How many faculty members have experience in constructing these types of courses? How many faculty members are willing to participate in these collaborative efforts? Are these faculty members from different disciplines, subfields, or concentrations? Are these faculty members willing to actively work in concert on this initiative?

The instructors in this departmental endeavor should agree, as a collective, on the selection of the courses within the department. The selection can come in cross sectional, sequenced, or hybrid form.

In the first form, cross sectional, identified courses that will participate in this initiative are those courses that are chosen across the disciplines, subfields, concentrations, or specialty areas within a department. Example 1: In the Department of Psychology, you may choose a course on research, clinical, developmental, and forensic psychology. Example 2: In the Department of

Business Administration, you may choose a course on business law, management, international business, and entrepreneurship.

The second form, sequenced, can be accomplished by offering one course per academic level, i.e., freshman, sophomore, junior, and a senior-level course (or introductory, intermediate, and a senior-level course), in one major or one field of concentration, dependent upon how your department is structured. Example 1: In the Department of Economics, you may choose a course on introduction to economics, microeconomics, intermediate microeconomics and managerial economics. Example 2: In the Department of Modern Languages, for a particular language, you may choose a course on basic and/or accelerated, intermediate, advanced composition, and conversation, and a Literature course.

The third or hybrid form can be accomplished by offering sequenced courses across the department's major or areas of concentration. This hybrid selection of courses will is discussed in greater detail under the section Departmental Model: Utilizing a Single Community Partner in Sequenced Courses.

Next, the number of courses that will participate in this initiative should be decided. As a guide, if the choice is the cross sectional form, a course from each of your sub-fields (or a majority of your sub-fields or concentrations) in the department should be chosen. If the choice is the sequenced form selection of courses, then either the number of chosen courses will be dictated by your department's sequencing of courses; or the department can simply agree to choose a total of 3 or 4 courses—one per academic level— introductory, intermediate, upper level; or, freshman, sophomore, junior, senior level; respectively. If the choice is the hybrid form selection of courses, a course from each of the sub-specialties/concentrations should be offered from your department, but these courses should be from different academic levels. Note that while more than 4 courses could be chosen to participate in this departmental initiative, increased time and collaborations for all participants must be weighed against the addition of another field of specialty.

Once the chosen form has been identified, the department should explore and come to a decision on the hours the students will devote to the experiential portion of their learning. If the department has agreed either on the sequenced or hybrid form, then the number of hours in each of the courses may be progressive. As an example, the department may decide to assign 30 hours to the freshman class, 50 hours to the sophomore class, 75 hours to the junior class and 100 hours to the senior class. If the department has decided on the cross-sectional form, then in order to avoid inconsistency amongst the courses and possibly students' angst, it is recommended that the hours should be constant across all of the courses in this departmental initiative.

The Departmental Course Creation Worksheet in Figure 4.1 is meant to be used as a guide in completing the selection and number of courses as well as the number of experiential student hours.

Single vs. Multiple Community Partner Considerations

As discussed in the previous chapter, for any course, a community partner should be a co-educator. Therefore, it is imperative that not only a relationship of mutual respect be formed, but that of trust—trust that the goals of the course are actually implemented by the community partner when the students are entrusted to them.

The decision to choose a single community partner or multiple community partners for your departmental initiative will depend upon a few factors:

1. The relationship already established by the instructors participating in this initiative
2. The preference (either through a majority vote or unanimity) from the faculty participants
3. The number of students and/or projects the community partner can effectively accommodate at one time (e.g., during one semester.)

Unless one of the goals of the department or institution is to expand community partnerships and while multiple partners can serve the goals of the course(s), department and institution, if a single community partner can accommodate a larger number of students and/or projects (i.e., to accommodate all of your department's experiential courses) at one time, definite advantages exist in having one community partner (as opposed to multiples). Some of the advantages of establishing one partnership for the department as opposed to multiple community partners are, as follows:

- The Instructors obtain a deeper understanding and appreciation of the partner's organization, mission, and goals.
- The community partner obtains a deeper understanding and appreciation of the Institution, its mission and goals as well as those of the department and the courses associated with the initiative.
- The community partner and instructors will obtain better comprehension of the overall abilities of the students and how to engage them in their experiential work.

Figure 4.1.
Developmental Course Creation Worksheet

Cross-Sectional		Sequential		Hybrid	
Courses	Hours*	Courses	Hours**	Courses	Hours**
Field 1		Freshman		Field 1 / Freshman	
Field 2		Sophomore		Field 2/Sophomore	
Field 3		Junior		Field 3 / Junior	
Field 4		Senior		Field 4 / Senior	
		OR.		OR.	
		Intro		Field 1 / Intro	
		Intermediate		Field 2/Intermediate	
		Upper		Field 3 / Upper	

* *Constant # of hours is recommended for all courses in all fields*
***Progressive # of hours per course's academic level is recommended*

Community Partner(s):

Notes: _____

- A deeper and richer relationship is forged in addition to "knowing the players."
- Increased open lines of communication and ease of communication among all participants are realized.
- Expectations from all sides can be better managed and upheld.

Student-Community Goals, Project, Experiences

After deciding on the issues discussed in the above sections, the choice of projects/experiences in the community must be established. These experiences must fulfill the goals of the courses, the Institution, and the community partner(s) and must be appropriate given the academic learning and level of the students. While each course within this departmental initiative may have different partners, experiential experiences, projects, deliverables, and goals, a consensus must be reached with respect to upholding the established departmental goals and the activity (ies) which each course will utilize to reach the departmental goals. Without agreement, a formal or direct departmental assessment plan, as discussed in detail in Chapter 6, cannot be effectively achieved.

Specific projects and goals may vary depending upon the chosen selection of courses and the length of time your students will be working with their community partner(s).

If your department has decided to employ the cross-sectional selection of courses and utilize one community partner, you may want to discuss with your department and partner taking on a project that can be accomplished from multiple perspectives/disciplines or sub-fields. In this case, each class can "tackle" the same project dissecting its causes and possible solutions from different perspectives dependent upon course's discipline/sub-discipline. The benefits to the partner will be a multi-faceted approach to the effective resolution of a cause or issue. As an example, using the Department of Business Administration example # 2 above, if the students' experiential work revolves around exposing the community to the topic of energy usage, the students in the business law course could research federal, state, and city tax laws surrounding tax credits and abatements with energy usage/efficiencies; the students in the management course could organize an informational session to inform the community about the issues/concerns of energy usage; the students in the international business course could research efficiency methods of energy usage in other countries; and the students in the entrepreneurship course could develop a business plan for local businesses to seek funding to reduce their energy intake.

If, on the other hand, your department has decided on the cross-sectional selection of courses but to utilize multiple partners, two approaches to the project may be undertaken. The simplest approach would be for each course to work with its chosen partner on a project, activity, or series of activities that fulfill the goals of the course and the organization. As an example, during the same semester, the students in a journalism course (where the course's goals

48

were to have students learn the art of investigating and reporting events, issues, or trends to a broad audience on a timely basis) could work with their community partner (where one of the organization's goals is to keep its customers informed of upcoming events on a timely basis) to develop and write a weekly newsletter. The students from the marketing class could work on creating a marketing plan for a fundraising event with their community partner.

An alternative, but a more complex approach, would be to have students collaborate on all projects from all partnerships. As an example, and in following the prior example, the faculty members teaching these two courses as well as both classes would have to work together (generally the students would be in groups) and partake in the successful completion of a specified project for each of the two partnerships. In this case, the students in the journalism and marketing courses would work on both projects—the development and writing of the first issue of a weekly newsletter for Organization A as well as in creating a marketing plan for a fundraising event for Organization B. For the first project, the marketing students can work on the actual layout and plan the distribution channel for the weekly newsletter, while the journalism students can concentrate on finding and writing the stories. Then they can work together in producing the final production of the newsletter. Similar separate but collaborative efforts can be applied to the fundraising event. The prime advantage of this model stems from the fact that the faculty and students will become knowledgeable in solving an issue or working on a project from different perspectives (disciplines)—cross-disciplinarity is advocated. However, this will require a high degree of cooperation, communication, time, and energy—on both the part of the faculty and students—and is not recommended unless the faculty members are experienced in conducting experiential courses and are willing to make this commitment to guide the students and projects.

If your department has decided to employ the sequential or hybrid selection of courses described above, and has decided to utilize one community partner, you may want to discuss with your department and partner taking on a project that can be accomplished in stages and/or from multiple disciplines. As an example of a project accomplished in stages within the same discipline, the students in an introductory mathematics course could assist after-school middle school children with their math homework while students in the advanced mathematics course could develop lessons plans and teach mathematics to the same children in the following semester. An example of a project that can be accomplished sequentially from the hybrid form, from multiple disciplines, is as following: Students taking the entrepreneurship course in the fall semester can work on helping Organization A in developing a business plan. Then in the spring semester, students taking the advanced accounting class can work with Organization A in setting up that organization's accounting ledgers.

In developing these courses, keep things simple; but at each stage, student responsibility and the level of the project's complexity and student deliverables should grow in scope and in intensity as the students progress through their academic journey.

DEPARTMENTAL MODEL EXEMPLAR: A SINGLE COMMUNITY PARTNER UTILIZING SEQUENCED & DIFFERENT-FIELD COURSES

Emerging through an institutional-written grant, Civic Innovations, sponsored by Learn & Serve America, whose goal is to allow "community groups and colleges to combine community service activities with educational, civic, or leadership objectives" (What is Learn and Serve America?) a hybrid form model from the Department of Business Administration was developed. The departmental model included one course at the freshman level, two courses at the intermediate (sophomore/junior) level, and one course at the senior level. For all of these four courses, one community partner, the YMCA of Greater New York, was utilized. The broad program goals were tied to the goals of Learn & Serve America, the broad goals of the YMCA, the broad goals of the college, the specific goals of the partners, department, and courses.

Specifically, for the freshman class, the identified course chosen to fulfill the civic engagement component was the Business & Society Reflective Tutorial. This course was part of the freshman learning community. These freshmen completed 30 hours of experiential service during the semester. They worked at the YMCA Virtual Y After-School Program. The goals for this class were to understand the concept of social responsibility and the interconnectedness of business and not-for-profit organizations. The outcomes were not only service to the YMCA, but an understanding of how students affect and are affected by the environments in which they serve.

For the sophomore/junior classes, three classes on a rotating basis were identified: Financial Accounting, Financial Management, and Consumer Behavior. These courses were stand-alone courses, not part of a learning community. The service consisted of 30 hours per student per semester at the Virtual Y After-School Program. The goals for the students taking these three intermediate experiential civic engagement courses were obtaining a deeper understanding of basic course principles while adapting classroom learning into age-appropriate activities they delivered to the children attending the diverse student-body of the YMCA. The outcomes were: discipline-specific lesson plans, games, and tests that the college students produced for the students of the YMCA.

You should have noted in the above paragraph that these intermediate-level courses required the same number of experiential hours as the introductory business course. In constructing the sequential course depart-mental model, a progressive number of hours for the intermediate-level courses are recommended; for this exemplar, this would have meant that these intermediate-level courses should have required between 30 and 100 hours devoted to the experiential component of the course. However, as these particular courses are required courses in the students' concentration and no material in the traditional-delivery course could be eliminated, the Instructors did not want to make the experiential component of the course too onerous. As such, the same number of hours required for the introductory business course was also applied to each of these intermediate-level courses. This is a case where student interests and practicalities of the curriculum trumped a model's theoretical construct.

Lastly, for the senior class, the identified course was the Senior Reflective Tutorial capstone course. (This is the same departmental experiential course that was discussed in Chapter 3, but with a different community partner and different projects.) Service to the YMCA included 100 hours per student per semester. Its goals included having the students gain real-world experience in doing a project, working collaboratively, developing a strong work ethic, and observing the dynamics of a diverse group of students. The outcome included many projects, among them: the creation of the inaugural Y After-School Newsletter; a Strong Kids fundraising campaign; the creation of surveys for students, parents and the YMCA's administration in order to improve upon its services; the creation of flyers for students and parents to promote the YMCA's offerings; and the redesign of the YMCA catalog/bulletin.

This hybrid model, Business Administration Departmental Course Creation Worksheet, is shown in Figure 4.2. Figure 4.2 is the worksheet from Figure 4.1 completed for this exemplar.

The departmental model was based on the view of experiential learning as outlined by Bringle & Hatcher (1996). The department organized the courses' learning activities around community needs and course content, and provided opportunities for the students to reflect on their experiences. The model met Bringle & Hatcher's objectives of: 1) a further understanding of course content; 2) a broader appreciation of the discipline; and 3) an enhanced sense of civic responsibility (p. 222.)

Figure 4.2.
Business Administration Developmental Course Creation Worksheet

----Cross-Sectional----		----------Sequential----------		----------Hybrid----------	
Courses	Hours*	Courses	Hours**	Courses	Hours**
Field 1		Freshman		Field 1 / Freshman	
Field 2		Sophomore		Field 2/Sophomore	
Field 3		Junior		Field 3 / Junior	
Field 4		Senior		Field 4 / Senior	
		OR		OR	
		Intro		Field 1 / Intro	
		Intermediate		Bus & Society 30 Field 2/Intermediate	
		Upper		See Notes 30 Field 3 / Upper	
				Sr. RFT 100	

Constant # of hours is recommended for all courses in all fields
**Progressive # of hours per course's academic level is recommended*

Community Partner(s):

_____   _____   YMCA Staten Island

Notes: _____

3 courses to be rotated: Financial Accounting, Financial Management & Consumer Behavior

ADVANTAGES TO FACULTY

The advantages to the multiple stakeholders involved in civic engagement initiatives have been expressed in the literature and throughout this book. While negative aspects, mainly in the areas of agreement and time, exist in developing and sustaining a departmental initiative, definite advantages exist that, from many angles, outweigh the negative aspects; and these advantages are heightened when compared with conducting individualized civic engagement courses. As argued by Lo Re, et.al. (2011), these initiatives have allowed faculty members the opportunity to develop interactive teaching practices as well as expand their knowledge and research agenda.

The following is a list, from an individual and departmental perspective, of the advantages in partaking in a departmental civic engagement initiative.

1. You are not alone. "Many faculty members express a sense of powerlessness on campus and a lack of clarity about their institutional role. This response comes in part from the isolation of privatized work, the disengagement of expertise, and a culture of discourse built on argument." (Campus Compact, 2003) Thus, faculty members involved in these learning modalities will no longer have to fear this "sense of powerlessness."

2. You have a ready audience off which you can bounce ideas, share the work-load, help in the handling of student and community partner(s) issues, and help with assessment.

3. Through faculty collaborations, it will increase your knowledge of other courses-disciplines.

4. You will have a ready collaborator or collaborators for your scholarly research.

5. You may have more fun.

6. It will increase the collegiality among your departmental members.

7. Approval and support from the Administration, Dean, and Department Chair will be easier with a group of faculty from the same department working as a team.

8. It may be easier to secure funding opportunities if a project is done on a greater scale as opposed to one class with one faculty member.

9. It will increase the service and civic exposure for your department.

10. The local press may be more willing to publicize a group initiative as opposed to a single collaboration.

11. Sustaining departmental representation in experiential service will be easier when there are many faculty members participating in the

initiative. This is vital as the faculty-community partnership(s) will not die if one faculty member decides to no longer partake in the departmental initiative.

Chapter 5

Indirect Assessment

This Chapter Contains:

VIEWS, DEFINITION & CHALLENGES OF ASSESSMENT
Tools of Indirect Assessment
CONSIDERATIONS & CONSTRUCTION OF INDIRECT ASSESSMENT OF
LEARNING GOALS: EXEMPLARS
Recap of Miller & Leskes' Assessment on Five Levels
Permission Needed to Publish Quotes and/or Data

As stated in Chapter 3, there are four challenges facing the effective construction of a community-based civic engagement course: the need for a mutual support system; changes in pedagogy and epistemology; integration of the civic engagement component into the course; and assessing the "value-added" of offering this type of experiential initiative. This chapter and the next address the fourth challenge—assessing "value-added".

VIEWS, DEFINITION & CHALLENGES OF ASSESSMENT

Starting in the late 1980s and especially in recent years, in part due to external accreditation requirements, virtually all state licensing-standard boards advocate and/or mandate that institutions of higher education have an assessment process system—the fundamental task of tracking, monitoring, evaluating, and making appropriate changes to improve students' learning outcomes. However, along this continuum, the view on assessment has changed— from being seen as a requirement to be met to being seen as an ongoing process for improvement.

Whether mandated or not, if assessment is done, the construction and outcome of assessment should be used for learning purposes. (Black, 2004) Thus, Assessment for Learning (AfL) can be considered any evaluation process that provides information to be used as feedback by instructors and students in assessing themselves and each other as well as to modify (for the purpose of enhancing) the teaching and learning activities. "AfL is a two-way interaction in that students use feedback from the instructor during the construction of their learning and the instructor uses feedback from students to customize instruction, catering to the apparent learning needs of the students." (Ludwig, 2011, p. 20)

Additionally, Wehlburg (2011) makes the case that assessing for learning does not have to be either for accountability to meet accreditation requirements or for improvement: "assessing for learning can be both formative and summative. And, assessment data is something that can be shared as a scholarly activity as part of the work done in the scholarship of teaching and learning (SoTL)." (p. 2)

So, if assessing learning is what faculty do—faculty research and then faculty teach; the students learn; and then faculty ensure the students are grasping what they want them to understand—then, as posed by Wehlburg (2011): "why is something that is such an integral part of teaching and learning considered anathema?" (p. 1)

Assessment challenges can be traced to human resources, finances, systemic practices, and the breakdown in communication. (Hollingshead, October 21, 2011) With respect to human resources, instructors are resistant, find it difficult, or complain that assessment is time-consuming. However, as argued above by Wehlburg (2011), assessment should not be viewed as a chore but as one of the tasks, similar to a syllabus, that will help guide student learning and teaching while meeting institutional goals and the community's goals and needs. Due to this resistance or inability to properly assess, many departments employ graduate assistants to create the assessment database, do the data entry, and run reports; many departments or divisions relegate the assessment responsibilities to a faculty or staff member; many institutions have hired a dedicated person or established a department to handle assessment; and many departments, divisions and institutions employ outside companies to create the platform for which assessment will be conducted. Such companies, databases, and exams include: Educational Benchmarking Inc., Collegiate Learning Assessment organization, Comp-Xm exam, and MAP-Works database. The amount of outsourcing depends upon the finances available at each institution.

The hardest and most time-consuming part of assessment is in its construction—establishing the goals and the tools needed to assess these goals. Once the assessment process and tools either for a particular course, a departmental series of courses (as in a departmental initiative), a program, or for an institution are established, it should take a limited amount of time to accomplish the assessment task(s). However, the challenge is that the practice of assessment is not done systematically. The inconsistency may arise in its cycle—when the assessment is done; the tool(s) utilized; and the assessment process itself.

Lastly, assessment challenges can arise in communication. While a particular instructor or department may have an assessment process in place, the outcomes may not be communicated to the individuals who need to know and/or have this information. As an example, a faculty member may decide to offer an experiential civic engagement course and use several assessment tools to examine the "value-added" of a particular project on the students and the community. However, once the course has ended and the data are gathered, the Instructor does not share the information with the Department, the Institution's Experiential Director, nor the Institution's Assessment Director. This breakdown in communication will inevitably cause an under-reporting of experiential civic engagement courses offered as well as project's outcomes.

Therefore, assessment should be manageable, systematic, ongoing, meaningful, and embedded in a course so as to inform program level and institutional level. Additionally, a communication plan should be in place to inform all constituents of their outcomes so that the impact from assessment can [and should] be viewed from the perspective of the student, the faculty, the department, the institution, and the community. (Gelmon, Holland, Driscoll, Spring, & Kerrigan, 2001)

Informal (indirect) or formal (direct) assessment methodologies can take place in formative assessment for learning—most often used in the classroom to make mid-course or end of semester adjustment "tweaks"—or, summative assessment for learning— and offer overall holistic judgment, deep learning. Both informal and formal assessment can be performed on one initiative. While formal or direct assessment is discussed in detail in Chapter 6, the attention to this chapter is on informal assessment.

What follows are: the tools of assessment and the considerations and construction of the indirect assessment of learning goals for projects described in Chapters 3 and 4. A sample Civic Engagement Assessment Questionnaire is also offered for your ready use. The last section of this chapter is devoted to obtaining written permission and using a release form (sample included for ready-reference) to publish student(s) or community partner(s) comments or project's survey results.

Tools of Indirect Assessment

Indirect learning assessment tools can be created and utilized to gauge the perception of the initiative/ program's strengths and weaknesses and its impact on students, faculty, institution, and community. So, what are the tools that can be used in assessment? The following are but a few main tools or activities of indirect assessment:

- Open-ended surveys—Example of an open-ended survey question: Explain how this experience has helped you understand the topics discussed in class?

- Closed-ended surveys—Example of a closed-ended survey question: On a scale of 1 to 4, how would you rate your experiential experience?

- Prompted interviews—Where interviewer asks (or prompts) specific and guided questions

- Non-prompted interviews—Example: recorded comments and/or discussions made by stakeholders

- Documented observations—By the researcher

- Experiments and performances

Indirect assessment utilizing one or all of the above tools can be used to show perceptions across (i.e., cross-sectional study) a group of stakeholders and over time (i.e., longitudinal study) to demonstrate how these perceptions have changed. However, bear in mind that dependent upon the indirect assessment tool(s) used, it may be difficult to show distinguishable progress over time. As an example, if you are utilizing the indirect interviews tool year over year and during the first year the interviewee responds, *I liked it a lot*; and in the following year another interviewee responds, *Most of the aspects were great!* is there a difference in these views? However, as an alternative example, if you are utilizing a closed-ended survey as your tool, then you can simply tally (or take the average of) the responses of scores. Nonetheless, irrespective of the indirect assessment tool or tools used to assess your project or initiative, these tools are valuable in measuring perceived learning outcomes and add another dimension of value to the quality of your program(s).

CONSIDERATIONS & CONSTRUCTION OF INDIRECT ASSESSMENT OF LEARNING GOALS: EXEMPLARS

Indirect learning assessment tools will be presented in terms of the two civic engagement projects described in the prior two chapters.

Notwithstanding the positive exposure, notoriety, and many compliments received at the completion of the civic engagement projects discussed in Chapters 3 and 4, for pedagogical purposes, these two programs should be assessed in terms of learning goals, and if possible, compared against the same course—in this case, the traditional taught Senior RFT course—without a civic engagement component.

However, in constructing this assessment, two issues should be addressed: the self-selection of students and the instructor for the two comparative courses. When the civic engagement courses were offered, most often, there were other sections of the same course that did not have an experiential civic engagement component. Therefore, to a good extent, the students self-selected to partake in the courses devoted to experiential learning. However, this was not always the case as, mentioned above, certain courses did not contain a counter-part; and students that were closed out of the counter-part course enrolled in the course with the civic engagement component.

With respect to the Instructor of the courses (experiential and non-experiential counterpart), for some of these courses, the same instructor taught both the experiential and the non-experiential course. When the same faculty member was not teaching both courses, due care in the design of the assessment plan was made.

In all cases, the Instructor teaching the experiential course took the lead in coordinating course goals and in sharing the assessment tools and plan for both courses. In the case of the Senior Learning Community Reflective Tutorial course, while the instructors for the varied sections were not the same, all Instructors teaching in the Senior Learning Community share one syllabus, and all aspects of the course are coordinated.

The perceived learning goals for the Senior Reflective Tutorials and the overall Business Department's Senior Learning Community can be assessed in many ways. The challenge was to choose an assessment method or system of methods that could truly capture and measure the perceived learning skills through this process. Keeping in mind that indirect assessment can be quantitative or qualitative in design, accordingly, an indirect assessment methodology, including four steps, was designed for these two projects.

Step 1. *Identifying and measuring specific skills— measured by the Civic Engagement Assessment Questionnaire—completed by students and community partners.*

An Assessment Questionnaire was designed asking students to evaluate seventeen skills and respond to two open-ended questions. (Please see Figure 5.1.) The skills to be evaluated were: Interpersonal & Oral Communication Skills, Ability to Work as a Team, Civic Awareness, Ability to Listen Effectively, Public Speaking, Ability to Analyze Situations & Information, Ability to Critique Situations & Information, Sense of Professionalism, Ability to Make

Figure 5.1.
Civic Engagement Assessment Questionnaire

Civic Engagement Evaluation

COURSE No. & NAME:_____SEMESTER:_____

ACADEMIC DEPT._____ FACULTY_____ SPONSOR_____

STUDENT OR COMMUNITY PARTNER NAME: _____

C O N F I D E N T I A L

	As a direct result of this course, please rate your skills in these 17 areas by placing a check-mark *(v)* in only one of the boxes to the right of each skill.	ABOVE AVERAGE	AVERAGE	BELOW AVERAGE	N/A
1.	PUBLIC-FORMAL SPEAKING				
2.	WRITTEN COMMUNICATION				
3.	INTERPERSONAL/ORAL COMMUNICATION SKILLS				
4.	ABILITY TO ANALYZE SITUATIONS/INFORMATION				
5.	ABILITY TO CRITIQUE SITUATIONS/INFORMATION				
6.	ABILITY TO PRIORITIZE				
7.	ABILITY TO ORGANIZE-ORGANIZATIONAL SKILLS				
8.	ABILITY TO THINK THINGS THROUGH IN STEPS-METHODICAL REASONING				
9.	ABILITY TO LISTEN EFFECTIVELY				
10.	ABILITY TO PROBLEM-SOLVE				
11.	ABILITY TO MAKE DECISIONS				
12.	ABILITY TO WORK AS A TEAM-TEAMWORK				
13.	CREATIVITY				
14.	STRATEGIC DEVELOPMENT				
15.	SENSE OF PROFESSIONALISM				
16.	SENSE OF LEADERSHIP/OWNERSHIP				
17.	CIVIC AWARENESS				

18. Please explain how this experience has deepened your knowledge of business and your particular area of concentration (Acct, Fin, Mkt, Mgt, & Int'l Bus.)?

_____

_____

_____

19. Any other comments?

_____

_____

_____

Use back side of paper for additional comments. Thank you.

Decisions, Creativity, Strategic Development, Ability to Organize-Organizational Skills, Sense ff Leadership/Ownership, Ability to Problem-Solve, Ability to Think Things Through in Steps-Methodical Reasoning, Ability to Prioritize, and Written Communication. These evaluative skills were chosen as they closely mirror the skills that employers seek in hiring business professionals. Therefore, in designing your questionnaire, you should select the skills which your field finds relevant as well as those that meet the goals of your course (or courses).

At the completion of each civic engagement project, each student and community partner was asked to complete this Civic Engagement Assessment Questionnaire in order to assess and quantify these 17 specific learning skills. Based on a 4-point scale: a score of "**1**" meant the student/community partner felt he/she had achieved an "above average" level of competence in that skill set; a score of "**2**" meant an achieved "average" level of competence; a score of "**3**" meant an achieved "below average" level of competence; and a score of "**4**" meant the student/community partner felt the evaluative skill was "not-applicable" to the project.

Once the collection of the questionnaires is complete, averages and standard deviations may be calculated for the student, class, community, and overall population. If the same questionnaire were given to the students at the end of the semester of the "comparable" class without the civic engagement component, advanced statistical testing can be done—such as t-tests —to gauge if any statistical difference exists between the two cohorts. Specifically, we can then ask the question, are the scores from the civic engagement course statistically better than the traditional course not devoted to civic engagement?

Step 2. *Identifying and measuring learning perceptions— extracted from the students' faculty evaluations forms.*

The purpose behind the civic engagement assessment methodology Step 2 is to formally identify, evaluate, and quantify students' learning perceptions.

As an alternative in designing your own questionnaire, statistical analysis can be accomplished by extracting the information directly from the students' instructor evaluations forms. Student evaluations of these RFT courses devoted to civic engagement and community partnerships offered during the single or combined semesters can be evaluated on their own merit or compared to the "traditional" instructor evaluations of the non-civic engagement business RFT course taught during other semester(s).

On the faculty evaluations, anonymously completed by the students at the end each of the respective semesters, students are asked to evaluate each statement on the evaluation form, on a five-point scale where: **1**=strongly agree, **2**=agree, **3**=neutral, **4**=disagree, and **5**=strongly disagree. Choose the statements from the faculty evaluation form that address learning skills. Example statements from one faculty evaluation form addressing student learning skills: *I have increased my knowledge of the subject matter; After this course, I am better able to understand how the subject is related to other subject areas; I have become more self-confident as an independent thinker as a result of the course; I have increased my ability to think critically and improved my problem solving abilities;* and *I have improved my communication skills (written and oral).* Please note that your institution may have a slightly different version of these evaluative statements/student questions, and you should always feel comfortable adding or subtracting (for the purposes of your analysis) any of the questions on the evaluation form (e.g., after all, these evaluative statements/student questions on the faculty evaluation form once the semester is over, are made available to the Instructor and may be used by that Instructor not only to evaluate his/her teaching effectiveness, but also to analyze and gauge a student's perception of any line item.) The drawback from using these Faculty Evaluations surveys is that not all faculty members are comfortable sharing their scores. Therefore, while the scores from these questionnaires can be extracted if you are the Instructor teaching the varied experiential courses or the comparable courses (courses with the same content but without an experiential component), cross-sectional or longitudinal compilation of data using Faculty Evaluation surveys with multiple Instructors may be problematic.

Step 3. *Compiling and evaluating un-graded, solicited and unsolicited comments—measured through the Civic Engagement Assessment Questionnaire's open-ended questions and by the students' reflective papers.*

Civic engagement assessment methodology Step 3—compiling and evaluating un-graded, solicited and unsolicited comments—can be measured through the written comments from the two open-ended questions of the Civic Engagement student and community partner Questionnaires.

The first open-ended question on the Civic Engagement Questionnaire (found on the Questionnaire's second section) in Figure 5.1 is: "Please explain how this experience has deepened your knowledge of business and your particular area of concentration (accounting, finance, marketing, management, and international business)." This question was designed to measure the students' as well the community partners' perception of how this experience enhanced the students' own field of specialization as is done in other traditional business Senior RFTs. As mentioned previously, in the traditional business Senior RFT, the students are allowed to choose their 100-hour practicum placement. Most students either continue the work they had begun in a previous internship related to their field of study or the students work closely with the Center for Career Development, to select a company and type of placement that will enhance their skills in the chosen field of study. With these two specific RFTs devoted to civic engagement, the students were required to work with their assigned community partners, and they were also required to work on assigned projects—relatively no choice as to the placement and type of project. Thus, this question was vital in the assessment of this undertaking, as it provided a measurement of whether the students felt these RFTs added value to their chosen specific field of specialization. Negative feedback on this question would mean the students would have preferred a traditional RFT course. Cited below, as a representation of what you may expect from a civic engagement course when asked this type of question, are phrases and words that were used by students when describing their skills and knowledge acquired through these civic engagement projects.

> Improved communication, presentation, interviewing, computer and public speaking skills; effective group work; opportunity to become decision-makers, creative thinkers; exposure to contacts in the business field, networking, high visibility; work with different personalities; "read" people; professionalism; personal input valued and taken seriously; telephone etiquette; learned not to take rejection personally; respond to difficult questions on feet; learned importance of compromise; became more open to suggestions; learned necessary everyday tasks are just as important in order to successfully complete a project; gains in marketing relation as well as real world experiences; benefit students in future, looks good on résumé, open doors to future jobs; able to hold an intelligent conversation.

While some of the above phrases were also articulated from students who had taken the traditional RFT course, *improved presentation, effective group work, opportunity to become decision-makers, creative thinker, high visibility, personal input valued and taken seriously, learned importance of compromise* and *became more open to suggestions* are phrases that were unique to the civic engagement designated practicum.

The second open-ended question found on the Questionnaire in Figure 5.1 is: "Please provide any additional comments." This question was designed to offer the respondents the opportunity to give unstructured feedback on the experience that may not have been captured in the closed-ended questions. Again, in designing your own questionnaire, you should rephrase the above open-ended questions or pose the questions that you want answered and are appropriate for your own course's civic engagement experience.

Civic engagement assessment methodology Step 3 was additionally measured through the students' unsolicited/unguided reflective papers on these specific practica. While the reflective papers can be formally assessed in terms of critical thinking for civic thinking (CT²) taxonomy discussed in Chapter 6, the synthesized comments can be used in ascertaining the perceived academic rigor of these RFT endeavors and in measuring perceived attained learning skills. As an example, the following phrases and words, extracted from the students' reflective papers, were used by students when describing their overall experience of these civic engagement projects:

> Found experience rewarding, fulfilling, has truly enriched my life both personally and career wise; opportunity of a lifetime; continued interest in the community, opened up a new sense in me, may look at economic development center in home area; forced me to look deeper into the area surroundings; broadened my education in a way that no other internships would have; worked on a real project with real results; became emotionally involved and attached; excited about the project when realized significance of the work; made me feel part of something.

These excerpts show laudatory comments and the depth of student involvement. In contrast, the traditional RFT experiences do not offer the students the same attachment and sense of ownership of their practicum.

Step 4. *Measuring interest by the community in having students' work in the community in future semesters— sustainability of relationship with community partners after the end of the course.*

Lastly, as a fourth step of the assessment methodology, it is important to measure the level of interest by the community partners in having your students' work in the community, interest, sustainability, and impact on the community evidenced. For the above initiative, this indirect assessment was carried out as follows:

- A short Community Needs Questionnaire was distributed when the students made their presentations to the public at the Sixth Annual Staten Island Economic Development Conference at the Hilton Garden Inn on April 27, 2004 and at the April 26, 2005 conference, to the community participants. Many inquiries were received showing an interest in having this type of civic engagement project repeated.

- The Small Business Association continued funding this project where it expanded its reach, in the following two years, in having the LDCs work with Economics and Political Science students.

- Based upon the work that began with our students on the St. George initiative, SIEDC was able to obtain a considerable grant from the state to initiate and continue with the revitalization program in the area.

In sum, the type of indirect or informal assessment you choose to employ is up to you. The above indirect assessment plan is simply an example of the types of indirect assessment tools that can be applied to a civic engagement course, some considerations and issues in employing these tools, how these tools can be used and analyzed, and some of the feedback you may expect to receive. You can and should alter you indirect assessment plan based upon your goals, the goals of the course, the institution and the community.

Referencing the departmental initiative discussed in Chapter 4, the department's goal was to assess the efficacy of this model with regard to Bringle & Hatcher's (1996) third objective.

To this end, in addition to a direct assessment plan for each course in the departmental initiative, explained in greater detail in Chapter 6, Section III, four indirect assessment tools were utilized: an indirect and unsolicited student writing piece and three surveys.

1. Student Reflections paper. A requirement for all students taking experiential courses, the students were asked to chronicle their experiences.

2. Perception of Global Concerns Survey. This questionnaire was developed to compare students' responses from same topic courses with and without an experiential component.

3. Perceived Skill-Set Survey. This is the same questionnaire as shown in Figure 5.1. It is used to evaluate individual student outcomes, summary course outcomes, and in comparing same courses with and without an experiential learning component.

4. Community-Based Learning Social Views. This institutionally-developed survey was used in comparing sophomore/junior and senior level student responses from students taking these experiential learning business courses.

In analyzing the above, the results of these four indirect assessment tools showed that students enrolled in these courses had a perceived enhanced awareness of themselves and their communities, as well as showed that these experiences had promoted student inquiry of broader global and social issues. In sum, these experiential courses showed heightened civic awareness. The questionnaires and outcome of this study as well as detailed discussions on the results of the analyzed indirect assessment tools can be found in Buddensick and Lo Re (2010).

Recap of Miller & Leskes' Assessment on Five Levels

In recapping the above indirect assessment plan for an individual course or series of courses, we can look to Miller & Leskes (2005) to see whether we met our assessment plan on five levels.

Miller & Leskes (2005) posit that assessment of student learning can be done on five levels:

1. Assessing individual student learning within courses (i.e.: What has a student learned—skill sets—over the course of a semester?). A questionnaire listing the skill sets you want to assess can be used to fulfill this level. Whether you have the students completing the survey in anonymity or not, you will still be able to evaluate each student's perceived learning skills.

   In the above exemplars, the departmentally-created Civic Engagement Assessment questionnaire in Figure 5.1 was used to identify and quantify the students' 17 skill sets per individual student and community partner as well as the community partner's perception of each student. (See Step 1. Identifying and Measuring Specific Skills above.) In addition, other learning goals were identified using the institutionally-created Faculty Evaluation questionnaire form. (See Step 2. Identifying and Measuring Learning Perceptions.)

2. Assessing individual student learning across courses (i.e.: What has a student learned—skill sets—in a particular major or program?) Indirect assessment tool(s) (i.e., any or all of the questionnaires discussed in the above exemplars, or other indirect assessment tools you choose to construct) can be completed by students in experiential civic engagement courses either across the discipline or program of study at one point in time or in sequenced (experiential civic engagement) courses throughout their years of study at your institution. However, to keep track of the students' progress, this will require students to be identified when completing the assessment tool(s).

In the above exemplars, the same Civic Engagement Assessment questionnaire was used across experiential courses to identify and quantify the students' 17 skill sets. Data for each student taking multiple experiential courses, whether in one semester or across all semesters, can be tracked over time to show progress. In addition, the Community-Based Learning Social Views Survey was used in the Departmental initiative comparing sophomore/junior- to senior-level student responses of those taking the experiential learning business courses.

3. Assessing courses (i.e.: How successful is this course in meeting students' learning goals?) A summary of the tool or tools used in level 1, above, will allow you to arrive at this question.

    In the above exemplars, summary outcomes from: the Civic Engagement Assessment questionnaire (both open and closed-end questions); select learning questions from the Faculty Evaluation questionnaire; solicited and unsolicited comments from students' reflective papers; and community questionnaire and follow-up were the tools used in evaluating an individual experiential course; results described above. For the departmental initiative, the results of the indirect assessment tools arising from the students' reflection papers as well as the three surveys employed, are reported above.

4. Assessment programs (i.e.: How successful is this program in meeting students' learning goals?) A summary of the tool or tools used in level 2, above, will allow you to arrive at this question. If you want or need to preserve anonymity of stakeholder's responses, you can assess this summary-level data with the same tool(s) distributed to the same content course(s) with and without the experiential component. This will measure the perceived "value-added" of the success in meeting students' learning goals for courses with an experiential component.

    In the above exemplars, the Civic Engagement Assessment questionnaire, Step 1, was again used to identify and quantify the students' 17 skills in comparable (i.e., same content course with and without an experiential component) courses; Step 2 Faculty Evaluation Questionnaire of learning perceptions was done but only with the same Instructor teaching the comparable course; Step 3 solicited open-ended questions with students completing the comparable Civic Engagement questionnaire were compared; and the responses from the Perceptions of Global Concern questionnaire from the departmental initiative results of comparable courses were compared.

5. Assessing the Institution (i.e.: How much have students learned over their time at the institution?). The same tool(s) can be distributed only to the designated experiential courses offered throughout all years of study whereby summary data can be compiled and analyzed.

    In the above exemplars, the Community-Based Learning Social Views survey was developed by the institution and was distributed to all courses with an experiential component. Therefore, a cross-sectional (per semester or academic year, department, course level) as well as a time-series or longitudinal study can be achieved.

While the indirect assessment plan for an individual course or series of courses (as in the departmental initiative) discussed in this chapter did meet the five levels of Miller & Leskes (2005) assessment plan, your assessment plan does not have to contain all five levels. As posited by the authors, while levels two, three and four are most likely used by the faculty as these areas look more closely at the connections between teaching within a course or a major and the learning outcomes that students meet, "identifying which level is being assessed in SoTL will help to better clarify the assessment work being done." (p. 3) After all, isn't this the aim of formalizing an assessment plan?

PERMISSION NEEDED TO PUBLISH QUOTES AND/OR DATA

The natural result of indirect (and direct) assessment, and as stressed by Wehlburg (2011) mentioned above, is to publish your findings. However, the federal government mandates that any research requiring human subjects must first be approved by your Institution's Institutional Review Board (IRB). Therefore, permission is required if, as an example, you want to survey your class and publish a quote from your subject's written or oral communication. Each institution should have an IRB and you should seek guidance and obtain approval before conducting any research on human subjects. You will need to bear this in mind when constructing your assessment plan.

Additionally, in conducting, presenting, and publishing your own research, if you are planning to use excerpts from the students' reflective papers, or directly quote students on their experiences, you should also obtain the students' written permission. Similarly, if you are going to distribute a survey to your community partner, in order to use their statistics or quote them, you should also obtain permission. A written permission form must be distributed to all human subjects involved in the study whereby the human subjects agree that the instructor and/or institution has the right to use any and all of their written and oral material associated with these projects.

A sample permission/release form can be found in Figure 5.2. However, before making a copy of Figure 5.2 for distribution, it is recommended that you first check with your institution's IRB or lawyer before disseminating this release form to your students and/or community partner(s).

Figure 5.2.
Permission/Release Form

NAME & ADDRESS OF INSTITUION

PERMISSION/RELEASE FORM

I hereby authorize *type in your Institution's Name* in its sole discretion, to use my name, voice, image or persona, or presentation or work, _____ of which I am an author for use in non-commercial postings on the domain, *type in web address of your institution* or other media outlets.

I authorize *type in your Institution's Name* to use my name and picture or works for which I am the author for educational, research, and promotional purposes. I assign any and all ownership rights I may have, including copyrights to *type in your Institution's Name*. I hereby release and agree to indemnify, defend, and hold harmless *type in your Institution's Name* from and against any and all claims arising from the postings on the domain, *type in web address of your institution.*

I have read and understand this document. I waive all rights to compensation for the use of my likeness, and understand that *type in your Institution's Name* will have sole authority over its use for educational, research, and promotional purposes.

_____   _____
Name (please print)   Date

_____   _____
Signature   Parent/Guardian Signature
                                                         (If under 18)

While your assessment plan should be developed before the start of the semester, you may or may not have decided whether you will indeed distribute a questionnaire, seek quotes, etc. Therefore, as a protocol and for safety precautions, you may want to have an approved Release Form ready and distribute the release form to your class and community partner(s) at the start of the semester, should you later decide to utilize your students and community partners' responses in the results of your study in printed form.

Chapter 6

Direct Assessment

This Chapter Contains:

FORMAL OR DIRECT ASSESSMENT DEFINED

Chapter 5 defined and illustrated the views on assessment and its challenges, and discussed the role of informal or indirect assessment in evaluating perceived measures of excellence for your experiential course or series of experiential courses. In creating your assessment plan, you may also want to consider, or you may be mandated, to utilize formal assessment. Formal or direct assessment provides a systematic way to evaluate how well students are progressing in a particular instructional course or program. Similar to indirect assessment, it can be used to evaluate cross-sectional or longitudinal outcomes. However, unlike indirect assessment - where dependent upon the indirect assessment tool(s) used, it may be difficult to show distinguishable progress over time - formal assessment is quantifiable; therefore, you will be able to compare the outcomes of your study to discern improvement or lack thereof.

In order to systematically evaluate a course, program, student, community partnership, or institution in a particular instructional modality, assessment tools are needed. Rubrics are the tools of formal assessment. Rubrics, once established by the Instructor and presented to the participants to whom the rubrics will be applied, are established rules that should be used by the Instructor to identify and assess the goals of a course or program. They are meant to not only clarify but also quantify the identified goals.

This chapter is devoted to the construction of a formal assessment plan for your experiential initiative; it is divided into two sections. The first section of this chapter, "Constructing & Assessing an Individual Experiential Course," provides sample experiential projects and gives you the tools needed to perform an assessment plan for the experiential learning portion of your course using one activity with several measurements or using several activities employing one or several measurements. Rubrics to assess critical thinking, civic thinking, content, and written and oral presentations are also provided.

The second section of this chapter uses all of the assessment constructs of the first section to augment and highlight a departmental experiential assessment plan and tools. The departmental initiative discussed in Chapter 4 is used as the example; but in its generic form, this assessment model may also be applied to any [departmental] series of courses.

CONSTRUCTING & ASSESSING AN INDIVIDUAL "EXPERIENTIAL" COURSE

As stated in Stiggins, "if assessment is…the process of gathering information about student achievement to inform instructional decisions, then the key starting questions for any assessment are, what decisions, who's making them, and what information will be helpful to them?" (2005, p. 1.) As discussed in Chapter 3, the fourth challenge in the construction of an experiential course is assessing and measuring the "value-added" of this type of course offering. Therefore, in trying to assess an experiential civic engagement course, the key question is, *is the experiential component of the course adding value to the students' learning?* The decision makers are *the Instructors and students.* "And, the information required centers on *where the student is now* in the progression of learning leading up to mastery of each academic achievement standard." (2005, page 1.) Therefore you, as the Instructor, must consider: what are the course's academic achievement standards? If you are offering an experiential-learning/civic engagement course, then you may look at assessing civic thinking and critical thinking.

So, how can we define civic thinking and how can we assess it? According to (Ehrlich T. , 2000); civic thinking represents an element of civic engagement and is what prepares students to participate in civic action. In order to assess civic thinking, the literature looks to incorporate critical thinking with civic thinking in a Civic Thinking Taxonomy rubric. (Critical Thinking for Civic Thinking. a) Based on the research tool, the Structure of Observed Learning Outcomes (Biggs, 1982), the civic thinking taxonomy is used to assess the civic development skills of students through responses to open-ended questions. From the consortium sponsored and endorsed by the Carnegie Academy for the Scholarship of Teaching and Learning—a collaboration between the American Association for Higher Education and the Carnegie Foundation—of six institutions, titled "Critical Thinking for Civic Thinking $(CT)^2$," the $(CT)^2$ rubrics were designed. The goals of this consortium and this taxonomy are to "better serve students by preparing them with the skills, knowledge, and attitudes that enable them to become critical and reflective thinkers with the skills necessary to be effective community, national, and global citizens." (Critical Thinking for Civic Thinking. b)

Rubrics for Assessing Critical and Civic Thinking

SOLO's Taxonomy for Critical Thinking rubric and the Civic Thinking rubric are reproduced below in Figures 6.1 and 6.2. (More details on these rubrics can be found in Critical Thinking for Civic Thinking a, b, in the Reference Section of this book and in multiple online websites. One such website is: http://www4.ncsu.edu/~damcconn/ct2_background.html.) These $(CT)^2$ rubrics are widely used amongst civic engagement practitioners. By applying these rubrics to an experientially-tied activity, from a scale/level of 1 to 5, where 5 is the highest, you can assess and score a student's performance both in terms of critical thinking and civic thinking.

At this point you may be thinking: *great, I understand the different levels of critical and civic thinking* (where Level 5 is the highest developmental level of critical and civic thinking), *but on which experientially-tied activity or activities do I use these rubrics?* This question can best be answered if we first take a look at the construction of an experiential project.

Constructing an Experiential Project

In constructing an experiential component of a course, as discussed in Chapter 3, it is common-practice to have students work with one community partner or multiple community partners on a topic that is tied to the course's content.

As an example of a broad and current topic that can be incorporated into the civic engagement component of a course (that may be assigned as part of a: finance, economics, political science, financial accounting, education, or

Figure 6.1.
SOLO Taxonomy

Pre-Structural	Unistructural	Multi-structural	Relational	Extended Abstract
Level 1	Level 2	Level 3	Level 4	Level 5
No understanding demonstrated - response does not address the question or restates the question.	Limited understanding of topic – response focuses on one conceptual item in a complex case.	Understanding of several discreet components – response is a collection of multiple items that are not related within the context of the exercise.	Understanding of several components that are integrated conceptually – response prioritizes information and is appropriate to the scale of the question.	Understanding demonstrated at a level extending beyond what has been dealt with in the question prompt – response generalizes to situations beyond the scope of the question.

(Used to measure critical thinking)

Source: http://www4.ncsu.edu/~damcconn/ct2_background.html

Figure 6.2.
Civic Thinking Taxonomy

(Lowest Level)				(Highest Level of Development)
Level Characteristics				
Level 1	Level 2	Level 3	Level 4	Level 5
Unable to state an opinion regarding civic action.	Recognition of at least one place for civic action or recognition of at least one interest or perspective other than their own on the issue in question.	Recognition of more than one possible place for civic action and recognition of the possibility of multiple interests or perspectives on the issue.	Provision of logical and defensible rationales for effective civic action through consideration of multiple interests and a variety of possible courses of action; inclusion of thoughtful presentation of arguments and claims based on an awareness of the variety of interests and the political and social context (a civic action plan).	Inclusion of all the elements of IV; in addition demonstrates the ability to abstract from the particular case; may include use of effective metaphors, the application of theory, or thoughtful consideration of similar cases.

Source: http://www4.ncsu.edu/~damcconn/ct2_background.html

even sociology course; dependent upon course and project's scope), is financial literacy; whereby the community partners may consist of several middle-schools in the neighborhood. Naturally, you can substitute any topic, community partner, and/or experiential component of your choice.

Having chosen the topic and community partners for the experiential portion of the course, bear in mind the type of questions posed previously by Stiggins 2005: *will the experiential component of the course add to the students' learning? How will you measure this? And, how will you tell if the experiential component did indeed add to the students' learning?* To begin answering these questions, an activity or series of activities must be established.

At this point, you have a choice: you can evaluate one activity using multiple measures of assessment, or, evaluate multiple activities utilizing a single or multiple measures of assessment. So, what activity or activities will you assign the class to enable you to assess the critical thinking and the civic thinking engagement component of your chosen civic engagement course? Will your course's goals extend beyond assessing civic thinking and/or critical thinking for the activity(ies)? If so, what are the other goals that you want to assess?

The rest of the chapter is devoted to exploring three activities: a reflection paper, a formal research paper, and an oral presentation. Additionally, the assessment goals for the experiential portion of the course in addition to critical thinking and civic thinking that will be explored are the communication skills of content, effective writing, and oral presentation skills.

Using a Reflection Paper as the Only Source of Assessment

As a primer, in addition to having your students spend time in the community, you may also want the students to reflect upon their experiences and write about it. Accordingly, you can create an assessment plan based upon a reflection paper.

With a reflection paper, you need not restrict your assessment to the Critical-Civic Thinking Taxonomy. You can further assess the students' papers in terms of content and/or writing. Therefore, your instruments to assess the students' reflection papers will be the Critical Thinking, Civic Thinking, Content, and Writing rubrics (where the Content and Writing rubrics will be presented later in this chapter). However, note that depending upon how you define a reflection paper (i.e., formal or indirect writing; short or lengthy; research-based or impression-based with or without support; required in addition to another activity or as a stand-alone), will dictate what instruments or how many of these four instruments you will use in assessing the students' reflection papers. So, what instructions will you give your students for this assignment? An example of the project's description with instructions for the reflection paper is found in Figure 6.3a.

Figure 6.3a.
Reflection Paper—Project Description and Instructions

PAPER/PROJECT ASSIGNMENT: "Financial Literacy in Middle-Schools"

This assignment will account for __"A"%__ of your final grade.
Minimum __"B"__ typed-pages

Instructions:
Financial literacy is very much in the news today and a grave concern for our youth and young adults. For your project, you will assume a hypothetical scenario: You have been hired by the New York City Department of Education to make recommendations about improving financial literacy at one of our local middle-schools (to be assigned during the first week of classes). Part of your research experience will include interviewing students and teachers at your designated school. You are to keep a journal and, at the completion of your experience, you are expected to write a reflection paper showing transformational changes in your thinking throughout your semester experience. You may incorporate themes from your journal entries. This paper will be assessed in terms of the following goals for this project: critical thinking, civic thinking, __"C"__, and __"D"__.
You should use the corresponding rubrics that will guide your score in each of the __"E"__ measurements.

In Figure 6.3a, "A"=the percent the reflection paper will count--out of 100% of a student's final grade; "B"=the minimum number of pages; "C"=content; "D"=writing; and "E"=the number corresponding to the goals you will assess. Please note that you need not include all four goals or measurements; the choice is yours.

Using a Research Paper as the Only Source of Assessment

In addition to having your students spend time in the community, if you want your students to do additional research on the topic of financial literacy (or your chosen topic for the course), a second common-place activity you can assign your class is a formal research paper. With a research paper, you can assess it not only in terms of critical thinking and civic thinking but also in terms of content and effective writing. An example of the project's description with instructions for the research paper is found in Figure 3b.

Figure 6.3b.
Research Paper—Project Description and Instructions

PAPER/PROJECT ASSIGNMENT: "Financial Literacy in Middle-Schools"

This assignment will account for __"A"%__ of your final grade.
Minimum __"B"__ typed pages excluding: Cover Page, Bibliography, and Attachments

Instructions:
Financial literacy is very much in the news today and a grave concern for our youth and young adults. For your project, you will assume a hypothetical scenario: You have been hired by the New York City Department of Education to make recommendations about improving financial literacy at one of our local middle-schools (to be assigned during the first week of classes). Part of your research will include interviewing students and teachers at your designated school. You are expected to keep a journal. You will also investigate the literature, and write a formal report making your recommendations. In your research paper, you must include at least five research-based solutions targeting your student population. You may incorporate themes from your journal entries. This paper will be assessed in terms of the following goals for this project: critical thinking, civic thinking, content, and effective writing skills. You should use the corresponding rubrics that will guide your score in each of the four measurements.

In Figure 6.3b, "A"=the percent the reflection paper will count--out of 100% of a student's final grade; "B"=the minimum number of pages.

Using an Oral Presentation as the Only Source of Assessment

Aside the students' several outside-the-classroom experiential hours at neighborhood middle-schools, if you want to have the students to research the topic, but not to assign any form of writing to assess experiential learning, a third common-place activity that may be used is an oral presentation. You can have the students hold a forum—present to their community partner(s) — whereby from the students' oral presentations, you can assess in terms of: critical thinking, civic thinking, content, and oral presentation skills. As a note, unlike a reflection or research paper where you can re-read the paper in terms of multiple measurements, oral presentations pose a challenge. While you may easily assess the students' oral presentation at the forum and possibly assess their content, it may be difficult to accurately assess the other two components at that same time. However, as a possible solution, if you were to video-tape or audio-tape the presentations, you can then replay the presentations and assess each student in terms of critical thinking and civic thinking as well as readjust, if necessary, your scores on the oral presentation and content. An example of the project's description with instructions for the Forum—Oral Presentation—is found in Figure 6.3c.

Figure 6.3c.

Oral Presentation—Project Description and Instructions

PROJECT ASSIGNMENT: "Financial Literacy in Middle-Schools"
Presentation to the Community

This assignment will account for __"A"%__ of your final grade.

Instructions:
Financial literacy is very much in the news today and a grave concern for our youth and young adults. For your project, you will assume a hypothetical scenario: You have been hired by the New York City Department of Education to make recommendations about improving financial literacy at one of our local middle-schools (to be assigned during the first week of classes). Part of your research will include interviewing students and teachers at your designated school. You are expected to keep a journal. You will also investigate the literature on this topic, and make a formal presentation to your community partner(s) based on your observations in the field, reflections, your research, as well as your recommendations. You may incorporate themes from your journal entries. While you may work as a group, everyone is expected to present. Your presentation will be assessed in terms of the following goals for this project: critical thinking, civic thinking, content, and effective oral presentation skills. You should use the corresponding rubrics that will guide your score in each of the four measurements.

In Figure 6.3c, "A"=the percent the reflection paper will count--out of 100% of a student's final grade.

Whether you decide to use one activity with multiple measures, or, use multiple activities with a single or multiple measures, the individual assessment rubrics and the assessment process are the same. What follows is an assessment plan for the experiential portion of a course using five rubrics (i.e., critical thinking, civic thinking, content, writing, and oral presentation) to measure three activities (i.e., a research paper, an oral presentation, and a reflection paper) in terms of a course's five goals (i.e., critical thinking, civic thinking, knowledge of subject, effective writing, and oral presentation skills).

An Assessment Plan for a Single Civic Engagement Project

Assuming, you decided to use the financial literacy experiential project cited above and assign a formal research paper, a reflection paper, and hold an end-of-semester forum for the community, incorporating the project descriptions and instructions from Figures 6.3a, 6.3b, and 6.3c, Figure 6.3d represents a project description and instructions for such a project.

For the oral presentation project example that follows, the students would not only be given a copy of Figure 6.3d—Project Description and Instructions—but also of all of the rubrics, so that the students would have a clear understanding of how they were being evaluated in each of the measurements and the activities; and feedback and adjustments can take place. As Ludwig (2011) notes: "Research has suggested that courses should go beyond evaluation to include aspects of assessment such as specific learning objectives, formative feedback to students, and adjustment of instructor practice on the basis of feedback from students." (p. 20)

Rubric for Assessing Content

Content can be assessed in all three activities—reflection paper, research paper, and the oral presentation. In order to assess content, you must first define what measures you will use to assess content. These measures should be closely tied to the project's scope. But whether you choose to assess content in all three activities or in just one—the formal research paper (as cited in the above project example) — you will need to construct a rubric. Figure 6.4, represents an example content rubric citing four measures and how each measure is to be evaluated and scored based on a 5-point scale; where 5 is the highest.

After collecting and scoring the research paper utilizing the Content Rubric in Figure 6.4, each student should receive a copy of the Instructor's scored rubric. (Note that in order for the rubric to be effective, the Instructor must assign a score to each of the Content Rubric's measurements; not just assign an average overall score to rubric.)

Figure 6.3d.
Project Description and Instructions

PROJECT ASSIGNMENT: "Financial Literacy in Middle-Schools"

This assignment, comprised of three parts, will account for 35% of your final grade:
- Reflection Paper (worth 5% of your grade)
- Formal Research Paper (worth 20% of your grade)
- Presentation to the Community (worth 10% of your grade)

Instructions:

Financial literacy is very much in the news today and a grave concern for our youth and young adults. For your project, you will assume a hypothetical scenario: You have been hired by the New York City Department of Education to make recommendations about improving financial literacy at one of our local middle-schools (to be assigned during the first week of classes). Part of your research will include interviewing students and teachers at your designated school. You are expected to keep a journal.

- You are to write a reflection paper showing transformational changes in your thinking throughout the semester's experiences. You may incorporate themes from your journal entries. This paper will be assessed in terms of your civic thinking skills. You should use the corresponding rubric that will guide your score. Minimum 3-typed pages.

- For your research paper, you will also investigate the literature and write a formal report making your recommendations. You must include at least five research-based solutions targeting your student population and may incorporate themes from your journal entries. This paper will be assessed in terms of the following goals for this project: critical thinking, content, and effective writing skills. You should use the corresponding rubrics that will guide your score in each of the three measurements. Minimum 10-typed pages excluding: Cover Page, Bibliography, and Attachments.

- Lastly, you will be expected to make a formal presentation to your community partner(s) based on your observations in the field, reflections, your research, as well as your recommendations. While you may work as a group, everyone is expected to present. Your presentation will be assessed in terms of your oral presentation skills. You should use the corresponding rubric that will guide your score.

Figure 6.4.

Project Content Rubric

	Not Acceptable 1	Barely Acceptable 2	Satisfactory 3	Accomplished 4	Excellent 5
Measures					
1. Solutions	Student discusses less than five solutions or they are not adequate in detail.	Student adequately addresses five solutions.	Student addresses five solutions in great detail.	Student addresses six solutions in great detail.	Student addresses seven or more solutions in great detail.
2. Research	Student relies on only a few sources or the sources show little validity.	Student relies on only a few sources but the sources valid.	Student incorporates a variety or many valid resources.	Student integrates a variety and many valid sources.	Student integrates a variety and many valid sources showing great depth of research.
3. Multiple Perspectives	Student fails to incorporate research targeting the specific populations.	Student somewhat incorporates research targeting the specific populations.	Student adequately incorporates research targeting the specific populations.	Student more than adequately incorporates research targeting the specific populations.	The student presents the rich diversity of the targeted student population.
4. Reflection	Reflection shows little growth over time.	Reflection captures the transformative nature of the experiential learning but no growth over time.	Reflection captures the transformative nature of the experiential learning with some growth over time.	Reflection clearly presents a case for the student thinking about the experience with evident growth over time.	Reflection clearly presents a case for the student thinking about the experience with superior growth over time.

By returning the scored rubric to each student, this will allow each student to obtain a better grasp of his/her strength(s) and weakness(es), vis-à-vis skills sets that were expected to be achieved for the project. Additionally, a summary of all the students' scored Content Rubrics (which can be set up in an Excel spreadsheet) can be compiled by the Instructor. If we assume we had 15 students in this class, Figure 6.5 represents the assessment of the class for the content portion of the experiential report.

Figure 6.5.
Class Content Assessment

Student's Name or ID	Measure 1-Solutions	Measure 2-Research	Measure 3-Perspective	Measure 4-Reflection	Student's Average
Student 1	3	4	4	4	3.8
Student 2	3	2	3	5	3.3
Student 3	2	1	3	3	2.3
Student 4	5	5	5	5	5.0
Student 5	2	3	4	4	3.3
Student 6	4	4	4	3	3.8
Student 7	4	2	4	5	3.8
Student 8	2	3	3	4	3.0
Student 9	3	3	3	3	3.0
Student 10	2	2	3	3	2.5
Student 11	3	2	4	2	2.8
Student 12	2	2	2	2	2.0
Student 13	1	3	2	3	2.3
Student 14	4	4	4	4	4.0
Student 15	3	3	2	3	2.8
Class Average	2.9	2.9	3.3	3.5	3.2

This summary-scored rubric not only will allow the instructor to see the class average in each of the measurements, analyze each student's average score across each measurement, but also see where (i.e., which measurement or measurements) the class as a whole was excelling or having difficulties.

From Figure 6.5, and as an example of how to analyze the above compiled content rubric class summary scores, it is evident that for the class, on average, Measure 4-Reflection is the strongest (average score of 3.5) and Measure 1-Solutions and Measure 2-Research are the weakest (same average score of 2.9). The students as a whole scored at the "satisfactory" level (class average score for all measurements of 3.2). Furthermore, Student 4 scored a perfect 5 in all measurements while Student 12 scored a 2 (barely acceptable) across all measurements. Naturally, if a student or students are scoring below par, extra help will need to be offered in some capacity; while if the majority of the students are scoring above par, more challenges should be explored.

Additionally, with the above summary-scored rubric, for the statistically savvy Instructor, you should feel free to do more calculations to gauge the level of your students' learning, such as: tallying the students below a score of 3 (i.e., not acceptable and barely acceptable) and students that score 4 and above (accomplished and excellent categories;) you can run t-tests to see if indeed there was a statistical difference in the scores for selected categories; etc.

Similar in structure, other rubrics can be constructed to measure other course's goals. As mentioned previously, for those instructors that may want to incorporate writing and oral presentation as part of a student's overall grade for the course, and in concert with the experiential project, sample writing and oral presentation rubrics can be found in Figures 6.6 and 6.8, respectively.

Rubric for Assessing Writing

It is a known phenomenon that with the onset of emails, instant messages, and the need to communicate quickly, the art of writing, grammar, and composition is quickly fading. Nonetheless, one of the largest complaints made by employers about our college graduates is their lack of skill in writing. If this is a priority in your class and if you offer a paper as part of your experiential component in your course, you may want to not only assess that paper in terms of content, but also on the merits of effective writing. With this in mind, Figure 6.6 is a sample of a 5-point writing rubric.

While Organization, Development, Style, and Mechanics skills are measures you may want to assess, "Format" may not be appropriate if the assigned paper should not be a structured or research paper. You should feel free to add and/or subtract the measurements as well as adjust what constitutes a particular score to meet your course's needs. Utilizing the rubric in Figure 6.6, and similar in structure as the Class Content Assessment in Figure 6.5, the class' 15-student summary writing rubric can be compiled for each of the 5 measures as shown in Figure 6.7.

Figure 6. 6.
Writing Rubric

	Not Acceptable 1	Barely Acceptable 2	Satisfactory 3	Accomplished 4	Excellent 5
Measures					
Organization	No hook; No thesis or thesis changes; Many irrelevant paragraphs included; No transitions between paragraphs	No hook; Thesis not tied to some paragraphs; Weak conclusion; No transitions	General hook; Thesis tied to most paragraphs; Transitions paragraph to paragraph	Original hook; No paragraphs not tied to thesis; Paper contains conclusion; Transitions par. to par., sent. to sent.	Gripping, non-clichéd general "hook"; Single focus; Artful introduction; Strong conclusion
Development	No examples; no detailed facts	Only one or two examples, one or two factual details within examples	Several supporting ideas; a few details	Variety of support; many details	Clear, logical, fluid, and subtle transitions, par. to par., sent. to sent.
Style	Choppy sentences, frags, run-ons, often interfere w/coherence; word choice and/or idiom usage often inappropriate; weak vocabulary; wordiness	A few sentence structure problems; word choice sometimes inappropriate; wordiness	Some sentence variety; appropriate word choice	Some sentence variety; occasionally rich vocabulary	Engrossing sentences; precise, effective word choice
Mechanics	So many errors in gram., punc., spelling, credibility is damaged	Many errors in grammar, spelling, punctuation.	Few errors in spelling, grammar, and punctuation.	Very few errors in spelling, grammar, punctuation.	Error-free paper
Format (ex: APA style for research paper assignments only)	No references or documentation Non-APA format	References are cited, but not appropriately	Refs to outside sources cited; entire document somewhat follows APA style format	Refs to outside sources cited; entire document follows APA style format	Refs to outside sources cited; entire document follows APA style format; completely error-free

Figure 6.7.
Class Writing Assessment

Student's Name or ID	Measure 1- Organization	Measure 2- Development	Measure 3- Style	Measure 4- Mechanics	Measure 5- Format	Student's Average
Student 1	3	3	4	4	4	3.6
Student 2	4	2	3	4	4	3.4
Student 3	2	1	2	2	2	1.8
...	...	...	...	...	...	...
Student 14	3	3	3	3	3	3.0
Student 15	3	3	2	3	3	2.8
Class Average	3.2	2.7	3.0	3.1	3.3	3.1

Analyzing the class' writing skills, you can see that, on average, the students scored below satisfactory level on Measurement 2 (class average of 2.7)—the paper lacked "Development." Armed with this information, as possible suggestions in improving this low score, you can: let the students know that this is a skill they will have to master, and follow it up with a class discussion on how to develop a paper; give students literature on how to develop a paper; bring in a guest speaker to talk about the principles of developing a paper; send students to a Writing Tutor/Center (if one is available at your Institution) with a note stating that the student should work on this skill; and/or in the future (next time you are assigning a research paper) incorporate better coverage of a paper's development prior to assigning the project and paper.

Rubric for Assessing Oral Presentation

Presenting information, making a case for change, or giving instructions are just three cases where the tools of oral presentations will serve students well. Effective communication is a vital component of one's portfolio if one is to succeed. While you, as the Instructor of the course, may not teach public speaking or cover methods of oral presentation in your class, you can have your students practice this art and give them feedback. If you choose to assign an end-of-semester forum or student presentation of their experiential project, you can assess several measures of a student's oral presentation. Figure 6.8 is an example of an oral presentation rubric that evaluates knowledge of subject in addition to 10 other oral presentation measures.

Figure 6.8.
Oral Presentation Rubric

	Not Acceptable 1	Barely Acceptable 2	Satisfactory 3	Accomplished 4	Excellent 5
Measures					
Knowledge of Subject	No theory anchoring subject matter; many errors; too few facts	Very little theory anchoring subject matter; a few errors; too few facts	Theory anchoring subject matter; a few errors; enough facts offered	Theory anchoring subject matter; no errors in facts; many facts offered	Mastery of subject matter; presentation flows smoothly; many facts offered
Correct Usage of Grammar & Language	No course terminology used; poor grammar; poor sentence structure; incorrect use of words; many slang words used	Very few course terminology used; poor grammar or sentence structure; a few incorrect use of words; a few slang words used	Course terminology used; good grammar or sentence structure; very few incorrect use of words; no slang words used	Many course terminology used; good grammar or sentence structure; no incorrect use of words; no slang words used	Many course terminology used; rich grammar or sentence structure; no incorrect use of words; no slang words used
Avoidance of Repetitive "hums" "okays" etc	Too many fillers--"Hums", "okays", "Ha-ha", etc.; too many repetitive fillers--"you know", "I mean", "you see", etc.	A few fillers--"Hums", "okays", "Ha-ha", etc.; a few repetitive fillers--"you know", "I mean", "you see", etc.	Almost no fillers--"Hums", "okays", "Ha-ha", etc.; almost no repetitive fillers--"you know", "I mean", "you see", etc.	One filler--"Hums", "okays", "Ha-ha", etc.; OR one repetitive filler--"you know", "I mean", "you see", etc.	No fillers--"Hums", "okays", "Ha-ha", etc.; No repetitive fillers--"you know", "I mean", "you see", etc.
Voice/Diction-Speed	Too fast or too slow; much mumbling	Somewhat fast or slow; some mumbling	Not fast or slow; almost no mumbling	Not fast or slow; no mumbling; some variation in speed	Not fast or slow; all words clearly heard; variation in speed
Voice/Diction-Loudness	Very loud or very soft spoken; no tone variation	Loud or soft spoken; no tone variation	Not loud nor soft spoken; no tone variation	Not loud nor soft spoken; tone variation	Not loud nor soft spoken; much tone variation

86

Figure 6.8. --Continued
Oral Presentation Rubric

Measures	Not Acceptable 1	Barely Acceptable 2	Satisfactory 3	Accomplished 4	Excellent 5
Eye Contact	Held audience contact less than 10%; only made eye contact with no or 1 person	Held audience contact about 40% or less of the time; made eye contact with a few people only	Held audience contact about 70% or less of the time; made eye contact with a few people	Held audience contact about 85% of the time; made eye contact with a good number of people	Held audience contact almost the entire time; made eye contact with a great number of people
Posture/Stance	Heavy slouching, rocking; hands in pocket and/or legs crossed entire time	Much slouching, rocking; hands in pocket and/or legs crossed most of the time	Only a bit of slouching, rocking; hardly any hands in pocket and/or legs crossed	No slouching, rocking; No hands in pocket and/or legs crossed	No slouching, rocking; No hands in pocket and/or legs crossed; command of the "stage"
Personalization /Engagement of Presentation	Monotone; no "connection" with audience; no "personality"	Somewhat monotone; some "connection" with audience; some "personality" shown	Not monotone; "connects" with audience; some "personality" shown	Not monotone; "connects" well with audience; much of "personality" shown	Not monotone; "connects" very well with audience; extremely "personable"
Appropriateness of Visuals (if applicable)	No visuals shown; or very poor visuals	Poor visuals; difficult to read; too busy	Visuals are "satisfactory"	Visuals are of very good quality.	Visuals are varied and of very good quality.
Interaction Among Presenters (if applicable)	No interaction at all	Some or poor interaction	A fair amount of interaction	A good amount of interaction	Seamless and effective interaction
Fielding of Questions (if applicable)	Presenter failed to field questions appropriately	Presenter at times failed to field questions appropriately	Presenter fielded questions appropriately	Presenter fielded questions in details in a clear & concise manner	Presenter not only fielded questions in details in a clear & concise manner but also proposed another position/ solution

Note that the number of measurements can differ from rubric to rubric. Once again, after scoring the students' oral presentations, the students should receive feedback. Utilizing the rubric in Figure 6.8, and similar in structure in Figures 6.5 and 6.7, the class' 15-student summary rubric of the class' oral presentation can be compiled for each of the 11 measures (Figure 6.9).

You can analyze the class' oral presentation skills in a similar manner as that of the other class' assessments. As a refresher, from this class' example in

Figure 6.9, on average, the class scored at a satisfactory level (i.e., 3.2) on all 11 measures with respect to their oral presentation skills. If you were to offer more than one occasion for students to present, on their second presentation (assuming you used the same oral presentation rubric), the class should score above a 3.2 for "improvement" to have taken place.

Many other permutations and scenarios of projects and their assessment can be constructed. In all cases, a summary experiential rubric—encapsulating all of the assigned activities, assessment measurements and rubrics used—should be constructed.

Figure 6.9.
Class Oral Presentation Assessment

Student's Name or ID	Measure 1- Knowledge of Subject	Measure 2- Grammar & Language	Measure 3- Repetitive "fillers"		Measure 11- Fielding of Questions	Student's Average
Student 1	4	3	3	...	3	3.4
Student 2	4	2	3	...	4	3.3
Student 3	3	2	1	...	2	2.1
...	...	...	...	...	...	...
Student 14	4	3	3	...	3	3.1
Student 15	3	3	2	...	3	2.9
Class Avg.	3.5	3.1	2.8	...	3.0	3.2

Rubric for Assessing Multiple Measurements

Lastly, whether you decide to use one activity or multiple activities, and if you decide to utilize more than one of the cited rubrics, you can construct a summary "experiential" assessment rubric. As an example, if you utilized all of the five rubrics cited - Critical Thinking, Civic Thinking, Project Content, Writing, and Oral Presentation - taking the students' average scores for each of the five assessment tools, a course' experiential summary assessment rubric can be compiled, as shown in Figure 6.10.

The construction of the Summary Assessment Rubric, as in Figure 6.10, is quite simple—in the top-column of your spreadsheet, type the name of the measurement rubrics you used in your class; in the row columns, type the names of your students that completed these rubrics. Note that for each student, the student's average score is reported in each measurement from that measurement's class summary.

Figure 6.10.
Summary Assessment Rubric

Course: _____

Student's Name or ID	Measure 1- Effective Writing	Measure 2- Project Content	Measure 3- Critical Thinking	Measure 3- Civic Thinking	Measure 5 – Oral Presentation	Student's Average
Student 1	3.6	3.8	4.0	4.0	3.4	3.8
Student 2	3.4	3.3	2.5	2.6	3.3	3.0
Student 3	1.8	2.3	1.7	2.0	2.1	2.0
...	...	...	...	...	...	...
Student 14	3.0	4.0	2.9	2.9	3.1	3.2
Student 15	2.8	2.8	2.1	3.0	2.9	2.7
Class Avg.	3.1	3.2	2.9	3.1	3.2	3.1

To illustrate: for the Summary Assessment Rubric, Student 1 had an average of 3.6 on the Writing Assessment (refer to Figure 6.7); had an average of 3.8 on the Content Assessment (refer to Figure 6.5); had an average of 4.0 on the Critical Thinking Assessment (rubric can be found in Figure 6.1). Likewise, the class' summary critical thinking rubric, while not shown, can be constructed in a similar form as other summary rubrics in Figures 6.5, 6.7, and 6.9; had an average of 4.0 on the Civic Thinking Assessment (rubric can be found in Figure 6.2), but the class' summary civic thinking rubric while not shown can be constructed in a similar form as other summary rubrics in Figures 6.5, 6.7 and 6.9); and had an average of 3.4 on the Oral Presentation Assessment (refer to Figure 6.9). Therefore, Student 1 had an experiential average overall score of 3.8—above average.

This experiential summary assessment rubric (as in the case of each individual summary assessment) can then be tracked over time to observe whether improvements in scores have occurred and in which measurement or measurements; as well as to observe what area or areas need to be improved. As stated by Stiggins (2005),

> *Research evidence gathered in hundreds of studies conducted literally around the world over the past decade shows that the consistent application of principles of assessment FOR learning can give rise to unprecedented gains in student achievement, especially for perennial low achievers. The implications for such gains for achieving adequately yearly progress goals and closing achievement score gaps are profound.* (p. 1.)

ASSESSING DEPARTMENTAL "EXPERIENTIAL" SYSTEM OF COURSES

The assessment of a departmental system of experiential courses is not all that different from the assessment of an individual experiential course. The difference lies in the summary assessment rubric.

Chapter 4 outlined a departmental civic engagement initiative whereby four courses were identified—one at each academic class standing—designing each experience to be richer and more meaningful, whereby the students' critical and civic thinking development skills and the content would grow over the four years. In an effort to analyze whether the students did actually achieve a higher level of civic experience commensurate with class standing, assessment tools must be identified and used in each of the four courses. For assessment consistency, it is imperative that the Instructors of these identified courses in this departmental initiative agree to institute a civic-engagement activity and employ the same rubrics. As an example, all the Instructors in each of the four courses could agree to assign students a paper to which the Critical Thinking, Civic Thinking, and Content rubrics would be applied. Therefore, each course from freshman to senior year, irrespective of experience, would be assigned a research-based experiential paper for which each Instructor would assess the paper employing the three rubrics (Figures 6.1, 6.2, 6.4) and then compile each of the class' summary assessments (similar in form as Figure 6.5) as well as a summary assessment rubric per course (similar in form as Figure 6.10).

If the Instructors for these four courses all agreed on this assessment plan, Figures 6.11a through 6.11d would represent an example of a summary assessment rubric produced by each Instructor of the four courses—from freshman to senior year.

Figure 6.11a.
Summary Assessment Rubric - Freshman Class

Student's Name or ID	Measure 2- Project Content	Measure 3- Critical Thinking	Measure 4- Civic Thinking	Student's Average
Student 1	3.4	4.0	4.0	3.8
...	...	...	...	...
Student 15	2.8	2.1	3.0	2.6
Class Average	3.2	2.9	3.1	3.1

Figure 6.11b.
Summary Assessment Rubric - Sophomore Class

Student's Name or ID	Measure 2- Project Content	Measure 3- Critical Thinking	Measure 4- Civic Thinking	Student's Average
Student 1	3.8	4.2	3.6	3.8
...	...	...	...	...
Student 13	2.8	2.6	2.7	2.7
Class Average	3.2	3.0	3.1	3.2

Figure 6.11c.
Summary Assessment Rubric - Junior Class

Student's Name or ID	Measure 2- Project Content	Measure 3- Critical Thinking	Measure 4- Civic Thinking	Student's Average
Student 1	2.8	3.5	3.5	3.3
...	...	...	...	...
Student 19	4.5	4.0	5.0	4.5
Class Average	3.7	3.5	3.3	3.5

Figure 6.11d.
Summary Assessment Rubric - Senior Class

Student's Name or ID	Measure 2- Project Content	Measure 3- Critical Thinking	Measure 4- Civic Thinking	Student's Average
Student 1	4.3	4.5	4.6	4.5
...	...	...	...	...
Student 17	3.7	3.8	3.9	3.8
Class Average	4.2	4.0	4.0	4.1

Note that the number of students per class can vary and will not disrupt the analysis, as we are only using class averages to develop the departmental summative assessment.

Once the classes and assessment for each class is complete, a departmental experiential assessment can be produced by incorporating each of the class' summary assessment rubrics' scores (from Figures 6.11a to 6.11d); see Figure 6.12. Of note, any series of civic engagement courses can be analyzed utilizing this assessment methodology.

The scoring methodology, reflected in Figure 6.12, will aid in identifying an overall score for each of the courses across all three measurements (vertical columns) so that the freshman class scored an average overall 3.1 "satisfactory" achievement across all three experiential associated measurements. The scores remained rather constant in year 2, but in years 3 and 4 this average score increased in every measurement.

Additionally, this same summary rubric (Figure 6.12) will aid in analyzing the average of each of the three measurements across all four years (horizontal columns) so that overall, course content received a higher score than civic and critical thinking; 3.6 vs. 3.3 and 3.4 respectively. However, if a score of 3 is considered "satisfactory" then all three measurements were found to be "above satisfactory" level.

Figure 6.12.
Civic Engagement Departmental Initiative
Summative Average Scores

(Based on a 5-point scale where 5=Outstanding)

Measures	Freshman Course 1	Sophomore Course 2	Junior Course 3	Senior Course 4	Averages
1. Civic Thinking	3.1	3.1	3.3	4.0	3.3
2. Critical Thinking	2.9	3.0	3.5	4.0	3.4
3. Course Content	3.2	3.2	3.7	4.2	3.6
Averages	3.1	3.1	3.5	4.1	3.4

Lastly, from Figure 6.12, the department's civic engagement initiative scored an average of 3.4 across all measurements and across all years. In the future, in order for improvement to occur in all three areas across the department (or any series of courses), this average summative score of 3.4 will need to increase over time.

Chapter 7:
Final Considerations

This Chapter Contains:

RELATING EXPERIENTIAL ACTIVITY, ASSESSMENT SCORES & GRADES
System for Converting Assessment Scores to Course Grades
CLOSING THE ASSESSMENT-LEARNING LOOP
FINAL THOUGHTS

The prior two chapters of this book have provided varied assessment tools and methodologies which can be used in their entirety, in part, or can be re-adjusted for better alignment with an Instructor's course's intent and goals, a department's goals for a civic engagement [initiative] series of courses, an Institution's goals, and the goals of the community partner(s). This brings us to the final aspect of the assessment and the teaching-learning process—relating the experiential activity(ies) and assessment scores to course grades, and the closing of the assessment-learning loop.

RELATING EXPERIENTIAL ACTIVITY, ASSESSMENT SCORES & GRADES

Generally agreed by civic engagement/experiential-learning educators, the external activities should account for a considerable part of a student's grade in order to underline the importance of such endeavor. Morris (1979) suggests that an experiential simulation may be most effective if it is the focal point of the course, and if it serves to integrate previous learning in the course. If the experiential activity(ies) is/are graded based upon a yes (completed) or no (failed to complete) answer, how can you be assured of the quality of the experiential activity(ies)? How much value did this experience add to the students' learning process? What aspect of this experience "worked" and which aspect did not? How can the Instructor improve on the students' experiential experience the next time this course is offered? None of these questions can be answered unless you have an assessment plan in place and you assign the activity(ies) a grade. While this is easily understood (and generally agreed) by most Instructors, some express concern that the theoretical portion of the course will take second-place if they place too much weight on the experiential component of the course. In response to this concern, keep in mind that as intimated by the rubrics presented above, from the same activity you can assess different measures. Therefore, you do not have to feel as if the experiential activity is "taking over" the theoretical course content. Furthermore, the above

95

questions may not be answered unless faculty members relate the rubric scores to students' grades.

The relationship between assessment scores and grades is not always understood. While many faculty members use rubrics and assign the appropriate score to each measure within the rubric, they fail to directly convert or use those scores as part of the students' grading system. The reasons the integration of scores and grades fail primarily arise out of misconceptions about their relationship or the utility of the scores.

1. The faculty views assessment scores distinct from grades so that they will assess (and use rubrics) for assessment purposes only and not integrate them into the individual student's overall grade for the course. You may hear an Instructor say, *Yes, I use the critical thinking rubric, but I don't incorporate it into the students' grades. I just score it and pass it along to the Assessment Director who uses it for assessment.*

2. The faculty views rubrics as only measuring a specific skill and, therefore, they are not directly related to the grade for a particular assignment or activity. You may hear an Instructor say, *Yes, I use the oral presentation rubric, but I don't use the rubric's total average score as the grade for the assignment, as it does not adequately reflect the entire grade for the assignment.*

3. The faculty believes that all measures in the rubric must have the same weight; therefore, it does not corroborate with the faculty member's weight in the grading of the activity. You may hear an Instructor say, *Yes, I designed the project content rubric and do use it, but I don't simply relate the rubric's average score to the students' grades; as I give more weight to their ability to find solutions versus the other measurements in the rubric.*

4. The faculty is unsure how to directly convert the scores from the rubric into the overall grading policy. You may see an Instructor that assigned two formal papers during the semester, applying the writing rubrics both times to the students' papers. However, on the first assignment a student received a score of 4.5 out of 5 but received a grade of 88 on the paper. On the second formal paper assignment, a student received a score of 4.5 and received a 90 on the paper.

In response to the four misconceptions about the relationship between scores and grades, or, the utility of the scores as they directly relate to students' grades, I offer the following rebuttal:

1. There is no point in assessing any aspect of your students' learning in your class unless you are willing to incorporate the outcomes of your assessment

tool(s) into your course. As argued previously, assessment should be used to inform and guide instruction. Therefore, the scores should be incorporated into the students' overall grades.

2. If a particular rubric does not adequately reflect what you are trying to measure in the assignment, then the rubric is flawed. You should be using a rubric that adequately reflects the goals for the assignment. Therefore, you should include in the rubric all of the measures that are appropriate and that align with the goals of the assignment. If you are using a departmental or institutionalized rubric, you can always add a measure or measures that pertain to your specific assignment, making that rubric work for you.

3. Just because a rubric lists, for example, four measures does not mean that all the four measures are worth 25% of the total score; nor does it mean, all four measures should have equal weights. In calculating the total score for the rubric, you can assign different weights to each of the different measures. Just make sure all the weights equal 100%. By using weights on each measure, you will be converting the rubric's total average score to a total weighted average score.

4. Some Instructors do not construct an algorithm, have not thought about constructing an algorithm, or do not know how to construct an algorithm for converting scores to grades, especially when involving multiple assessment tools. In response, the following methodology is offered.

System for Converting Assessment Scores to Course Grades

To concretize the above, let's say you wanted to construct a grading methodology where about one third of a student's overall grade is devoted to the experiential components of the course. So, what activity or activities will you assign the class to enable you to assess the experiential component of the course? As an example, and in concert with a slight variation with the exposition of the above tools, I propose three common-place activities for the experiential component of the course: a research paper, a reflection paper, and an oral presentation. (Note: A variation is shown to illustrate the flexibility in which you can "select" the various combination of assessment tools per activity employed.)

You can assign a research paper, worth 20% of a student's overall grade; incorporating research on a particular topic from your course's content and as it is evidenced in the external experience component of the course. With the same instrument, the research paper, you can assess it in terms of: critical thinking, civic thinking, content, and/or writing. For sake of simplicity, if you take the position that each has an equal weight in the overall grade, then each component will account for 5% of the research paper's grade (i.e., 4 components @ 5% each = 20%; or 4 components @ 4 points each = the maximum 20 points value established for the research paper). If you use the associated 5-point rubrics (or a version of the rubrics) in assessing each of the components, then if "Student X" received an average total score of 3.3 on the Critical Thinking Rubric, an average total score of 4.0 on the Civic Thinking Rubric, an average total score of 4.5 on the Content Rubric, and an average total score of 3.7 on the Writing Rubric, then "Student X's" grade on the research paper would equal 15.5 points (out of a potential 20 points).

You can additionally have students present their research papers (oral presentation) worth 10% of a student's overall grade. With the oral presentation, you can assess it in terms of presentation and/or content. For sake of simplicity, if you take the position that content was already assessed in the research paper and note that "knowledge of subject" is one of the measurements in the Oral Presentation Rubric, then the entire oral presentation component will account for 10% of the grade. If you use the associated 5-point rubric (or a version of the rubric from Chapter 6) in assessing this component, you can simply double the total average student's achieved score. Example, if a student received an average total score of 4.5 on the Oral Presentation Rubric, then the student's grade on the presentation would equal 9% (out of a potential 10%).

Lastly, you can assign a reflection paper, worth 5% of a student's overall grade. With the reflection paper, similar to the research paper, you can assess it in terms of: critical thinking, civic thinking, content, and/or writing. However, note that as stated previously, how you define a reflection paper (i.e., formal or indirect writing; short or lengthy; research-based or impression-based with or without support; required in addition to a formal research paper or as a stand-alone) will dictate the percent of the grade and what instruments or how many of these 4 instruments you will use in assessing this reflection paper. For sake of simplicity, if you take the position that you will use the reflection paper to only assess content and civic thinking, and if you use the associated 5-point rubrics (or a version of the rubrics from Chapter 6) in assessing these components, you can simply take the average of the total average student's achieved scores in both rubrics. Example, if a student received an average total score of 4.5 on the Civic Thinking Rubric and received an average total score of 3.5 on the Content Rubric, then the student's grade on the reflection paper would equal 4% (i.e., [4.5 + 3.5] / 2) out of a potential 5%.

We can summarize the above-cited student's 35% of his/her total grade devoted to the experiential component of the course (whereby the rest of the course's grading, 65%, can be devoted to pure course content and assessed through exams, etc.). For this student, 20% was devoted to assess a research paper, 5% was devoted to assess a reflection paper, and 10% was devoted to assess oral presentation. In the above scenario, utilizing the rubrics and outcomes above, this student earned 15.5%, 4% and 9% respectively, for a total of 28.5% out of a maximum 35% (or 28.5 points to be applied to the course points of 100).

A grading book (which can be created in Excel) incorporating a student's experiential scores and grade equivalences along with sample activities' scores and grade equivalences of the non-experiential portion of the course can be compiled along the lines of Figure 7.1.

CLOSING THE ASSESSMENT-LEARNING LOOP

Whether you favor using direct, indirect, or a combination of both direct and indirect assessment for the formative or summative reporting of your course or courses, ideally, there are 11 steps in the assessment process.

The first step is to identify the goals of the initiative. For example, this course will increase the students' skills in [fill in the skills]; or the students will be able to [fill in the proficiencies]. The second step is to decide what you want to assess. Which of these goals or proficiencies will you assess? Not all goals or proficiencies need to be assessed during one semester; they can be assessed on a systematic cycle. The third step is to create an assessment plan based upon step 2. This includes the decision of whether you want to use direct or indirect measures of assessment and which tools to use. Then, in step 4, you should design your tools for assessment or adopt a department's or institution's assessment tools that can measure your stated goals. Your fifth step would be to gather the data. The gathering of the data may include the distribution and graded rubric(s), distribution and collection of surveys, quotes, etc. Certainly all instructors that are mandated to conduct assessment as well as those that elect to undergo assessment would most likely perform these first 5 steps or some semblance of these steps.

This brings us to step 9. Either in isolation, or in collaboration with other members, you need to decide what worked and thus needs to continue; what worked with minor kinks and thus needs to be modified; and, what did not work and thus needs to be totally re-worked or eliminated. This practice is needed to inform teaching and learning decisions. Step 10 involves the process of including these decisions and changes into your curriculum—closing of the loop. This is what makes assessment a transformative process. Transformative assessment is a process that will "inform decision making that is appropriate, meaningful, sustainable, flexible and ongoing," which will enhance the effectiveness in your institution. (Welhburg, 2011, p. 4)

Figure 7.1.
Student Grading Book

ACTIVITIES	RUBRICS	SCORES	GRADE EQUIVALENTS	FINAL GRADE
Research Paper (20%)	Content (5%)	4.5		
	Civic Thinking (5%)	4.0		
	Critical Thinking (5%)	3.3		
	Writing (5%)	3.7		
Percentage Points			15.5	
Oral Presentation (10%)	Oral Presentation (5%)	4.5		
Percentage Points			9.0	
Reflection Paper (5%)	Civic Thinking (5%)	4.5		
	Content (5%)	3.5		
Percentage Points			4.0	
Sub-Total of Experiential Component (out of 35%)		=======>	==========>	**28.5**
Midterm Exam (25%)	Written Exam	89.0	22.25	
Final Exam (30%)	Written Exam	91.0	27.3	
Class Participation (10%)			9.5	
Sub-Total of Non-Experiential Component (out of 65%)		=====>	==========>	**59.05**
FINAL STUDENT GRADE				**87.55**

The last step in this process, as espoused in Chapter 5 as challenge #4 of assessment, is to share your data with all constituents at your institution that need to be aware of your assessment outcome.

While assessment is created for the purpose of providing individual course, program, or Institutional-level information, in order to enhance learning, Wehlburg (2011) stresses that in addition to this goal, we should have a 12th step in the assessment process pyramid—making assessment part of the larger SoTL literature. "Assessment is indeed a scholarly process that plays a crucial role in the ongoing conversations about teaching and learning. Assessment is more than a service activity; it is scholarly work that should be publically shared and discussed." (Welhburg, 2011, p. 5) She argues that by publishing the results of our assessment work, not only will the body of knowledge about learning and assessment be shared amongst our colleagues and grow, but "we can also help those outside of academia to better understand the goals, outcomes, and the overall learning that occurs at the college level." (p. 5)

Figure 7.2 shows the 12 assessment steps in pyramid form to illustrate not only the hierarchical nature of these steps, but also to (unfortunately) illustrate the number of faculty members that reach each level of the pyramid on the "climb" to the top!

While the assessment process an Instructor may use may vary, direct or indirect assessment should be systematic, ongoing, and meaningful in order to impact reform at the course, program, and institutional level.

Additionally, irrespective of the Instructor's decision to publish his/her findings in the academic literature, Step 12 of the Assessment Process, one thing in assessment is certain: if thought out and done properly, assessment is a powerful tool not only for the Instructor, the department, the institution, and the community, but also for the student—higher education's prime concern.

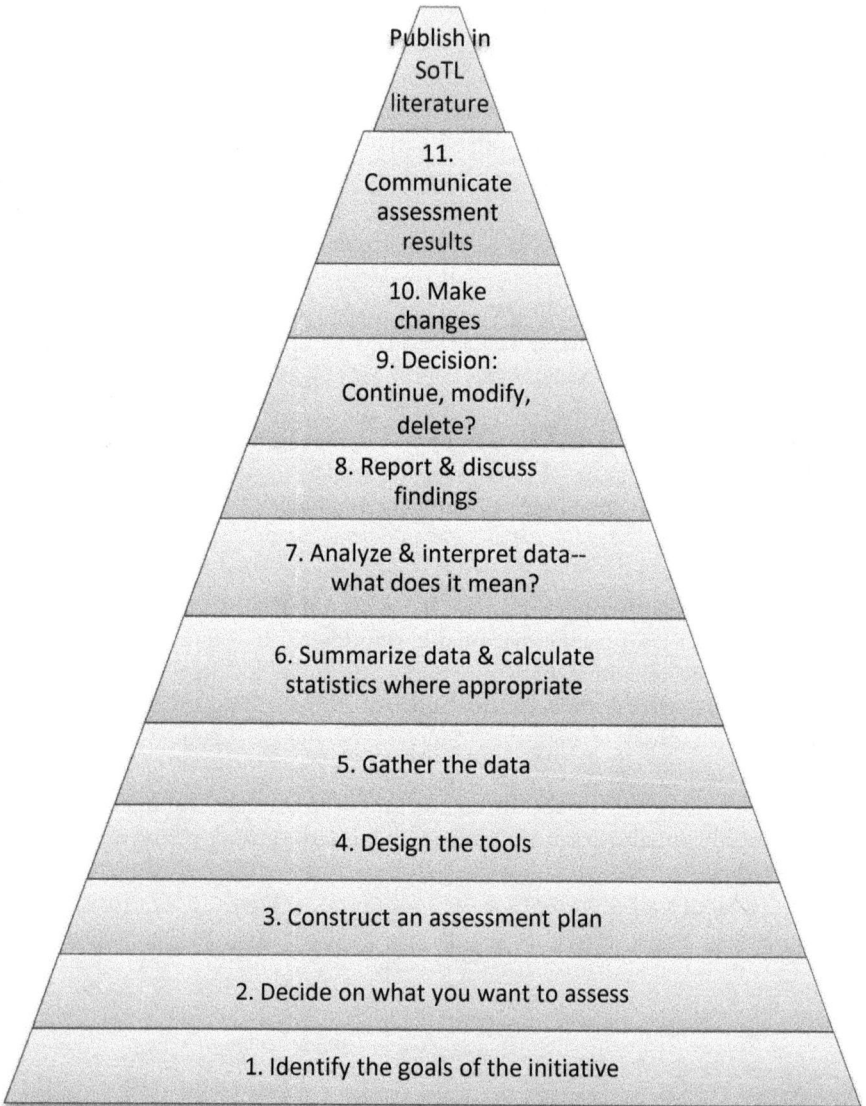

Figure 7.2.
The Assessment Process

Publish in SoTL literature

11. Communicate assessment results

10. Make changes

9. Decision: Continue, modify, delete?

8. Report & discuss findings

7. Analyze & interpret data-- what does it mean?

6. Summarize data & calculate statistics where appropriate

5. Gather the data

4. Design the tools

3. Construct an assessment plan

2. Decide on what you want to assess

1. Identify the goals of the initiative

FINAL THOUGHTS

The resurgence of experiential or civic engagement models has been a response to three main critiques:

1. A need to improve student learning

2. Lack of critical thinking skills

3. Lack of civic awareness and responsibility

While the creation of an experiential civic engagement course or system of courses, within a learning community or as stand-alone courses, involving reflective practices and community partners may not entirely eradicate these three issues in higher education, research with both indirect and direct assessment of these initiatives shows that these models do work in addressing these critiques. Therefore, this book is not only written to serve as a resource, as well as offer new tools to experienced practitioners of this field of study, but also to encourage new faculty, departments, and administrators to join this new curricula initiative.

In applying some of guidelines expressed in this book to your initiative, please feel free to pick and choose, or alter the material in order to more appropriately meet the goals of your course, your department, your community partner(s), and/or your institution.

Lastly, and most importantly, as we are all working toward the same goals in educating our students, do not hesitate to contact me with any comments, questions, concerns, or new practices, studies or theories in this field you wish to share.

I hope you will find the same fulfillment as I have found in transitioning from "traditional" classroom teaching to utilizing reflective, experiential, civic engagement practices, preferably as part of a learning community and co-educating community partners.

REFERENCES

Barr, J., & Tagg, R. B. (1995). "From Teaching to Learning-a New Paradigm for Undergraduate Education". *Change*, 27(6), 12-25.

Basinger, N., & Bartholomew, K. (2006). "Service-learning in nonprofit organizations: Motivations, expectations, and outcomes". *Michigan Journal of Community Service-learning*, 12(2), 15-26.

Bath, C. S. (2006). "The Role of the Learning Community in the Development of Discipline Knowledge and Generic Graduate Outcomes". *Higher Education*, 259-286.

Benson, L., & Harkavy, I. (2001). "Leading the way to meaningful partnerships". *Principal Leadership*, 2(1), 54-58.

Biggs, J. B. (1982). *Evaluating the Quality of Learning: The SOLO Taxonomy*. Academic Press.

Black, P., C. Harrison, C. Lee, B.; Marshall, and D. Wiliam. (2004). "Working inside the black box: Assessment for learning in the classroom". *Phi Delta Kappan*, 86(1): *8–21*.

Boud, D., Keogh, R., Walker, D. (1985). *Reflections: turning experience into learning.* Published in 1985 by Nichols Publishing Co., NY) reprinted by Routledge-Falmer, Taylor & Francis Group, 1994, pg. 18.

Boyd, E. M. & Fales, A.W. (1983). "Reflective Learning Key to Learning from Experience". *Journal of Humanistic Psychology. Spring*, 23(2), 99-117.

Bringle, R. G. & Hatcher, J. A. (1996). "Implementing service-learning in higher education". *Journal of Higher Education*, 67(2), 221-239.

Buddensick, Janice & Mary Lo Re. (October 2010) *"Measuring the Effect of Service-learning on Civic Awareness"* Review of Business Research, EBSCO Publishing & Gale Group/Thompson Publishing, MS, Vol. 5, No. 5, pages 101-7.

Business Administration Senior Program. (n.d.). Retrieved March 19, 2009, from Wagner College: http://www.wagner.edu/media/node/44

Campus Compact. (2010). *Annual Membership Survey Executive Summary.* Retrieved September 18, 2011, from Campus Compact: http://www.compact.org/about/statistics/

Campus Compact. (2003). *Introduction to Service-Learning Toolkit: Readings & Resources for Faculty.* Campus Compact.

CCPH. (1999). *Community-Campus Partnerships for Health, Principles and best practices for healthier communities.* Conference Proceedings. April 25-28, 1998, Pittsburgh, PA. Retrieved from http://depts.washington.edu/ ccph/pdf_files/98PROCED.pdf.

Citizen Scholar. (n.d.). Retrieved March 19, 2009, from Center for Civic Engagement: http://www.stpt.usf.edu/community

Coleman, J.S. (1976). *Differences between Experiential and Classroom Learning. Experiential Learning,*Washington: Jossey-Bass Publishers, 1976, 49-61.

College Seniors Give Reports on Local Involvement. (2005, April 27). The Staten Island Advance, p. A26.

Critical Thinking for Civic Thinking. a. (n.d.). Retrieved March 23, 2010, from http://www4.ncsu.edu/~damcconn/ct2_research.html

Critical Thinking for Civic Thinking. b. (n.d.). Retrieved March 24, 2010, from http://www.cfkeep.org/html/snapshort.php?id=9952780706764

Dewey, John (1916) *Democracy and Education: An Introduction to the Philosophy of Education.* Cornell University Library Pub. Reprinted August 2009.

Dewey, John (1933) *Essays on How we Think.Southern.* Illinois University Press reprinted in January 1986.

Dewey, J. (1944). *Democracy and education.* New York: Free Press.

Eatman, J. E. (2008). *Scholarship in Public: Knowledge Creation and Tenure Policy in the Engaged University.* Imagining America, p. 26.

Ehrlich, T. (2000). *Civic Responsibility and Higher Education.* Phoenix: Oryx Press.

Encyclopedia Brunoniana. (1993). *Facts: Alexander Meiklejohn.* Retrieved October 11, 2011, from Brown University Library: http://brown.edu/Administration/News_Bureau/Encyclopedia/Meiklejohn.ht ml

First-Year Freshman Learning Community. (n.d.). Retrieved March 19, 2009, from Wagner College: http://www.wagner.edu/experiential_learning/FYP

Freire, P. (1970). "The Banking Concept of Education", in P. Freire, *Pedagogy of the Oppressed.* New York: Continuum Books; reprinted in 1993.

Furco, A. (1996). "Service-Learning: A Balanced Approach to Experiential Education". In *Expanding Boundaries: Service and Learning* (pp. 2-6). Washington DC: Corporation for National Service.

Gelmon, S. B., Holland, B. A., Seifer, S. D., Shinnamon, A., & Connors, K. (1998a). "Community-university partnerships for mutual learning". *Michigan Journal of Community Service-learning,* 5, 97-107.

Gelmon, S. B., Holland, B. A., & Shinnamon, A. F. (1998b). *Health profession schools in service to the nation,* 1996-1998 final evaluation report. Portland, OR: Portland State University.

Guarasci, Richard. (2012) A Crucible Moment. White House, Washington, DC.

Hollingshead, B. (October 21, 2011). *Assessing First-Year Learning Communities,* Learning Communities & the First-Year Student 11th Annual ACLC Retreat. West Hartford, CT.

Inspired to Serve. (n.d.). *Identifying Funding to Sustain Your Efforts.* Retrieved September 18, 2011, from Inspired to Serve: http://www.inspiredtoserve.org/funding

Intermediate Learning Community. (n.d.). Retrieved March 19, 2009, from Wagner College: http://wagner.edu/experiential_learning/ILC

Island Business Leaders Keep the Economy Moving. (2004, March 28). The Staten Island Advance, p. A11.

Jones, S. (2003). "Introduction to the Second Edition", in C. Compact, *Introduction to Service-Learning Toolkit: Readings and Resources for Faculty* (p. 1). MA: Campus Compact.

Kuh, G. D. (2008). *High-impact educational practices: What they are, who has access to them, and why they matter.* Washington, D.C.: Association of American Colleges & Universities.

Leiderman, S., Furco, A., Zapf, J., & Goss, M. (2003). *Building partnerships with college campuses: Community perspectives,* a monograph. Washington, DC: Council of

Independent Colleges/Consortium for the Advancement of Private Higher Education.

Lo Re, M. L. (2004, October Vol. 15, No. 4). "St. George Action Plan-A Civic Engagement Endeavor". *Metropolitan Universities Journal, an International Forum*, pp. 85-98.

Lo Re, M. L. (2004, October 5). *St. George Action Plan--A Civic Engagement Endeavor*. Coalition of Urban & Metropolitan Universities, New York City, NY.

Lo Re, M., DeSimone, F., & Buddensick, J. (2011, Vol. 11 No. 3). "Engaged Learning Models for Civic Engagement". *European Journal of Management*, pp. 79-87.

Ludwig, M., Bentz, A., & Fynewever, H.. (2011). "Your Syllabus Should Set the Stage for Assessment for Learning". *Journal of College Science Teaching*, 40(4), 20-23. Retrieved July 18, 2011, from ProQuest Education Journals. (Document ID: 2306052961).

Merriam, S. B. (1998). "Qualitative Research and Case Study Applications in Education". *Revised and Expanded from "Case Study Research in Education*. San Francisco: Jossey-Bass Publishers.

Mihalynuk, T. V., & Seifer, S. D. (2002, September, 2002). *Partnerships for higher education service-learning*. Retrieved from http://www.service-learning.org/ resources/fact_sheets/he_facts/he_partners.

Miller, R., & Leskes, A. (2005). *Levels of Assessment: From the Student to the Institution*. The Association of American Colleges and Universities, 1-15.

Morris, C. 1979. "Simulation evaluation designs", in *Simulations in higher education*, ed. E. Thorson. Hicksville, N.Y.: Exposition.

NSLLP. (n.d.). Retrieved October 21, 2011, from National Studies of Living Learning Programs: http://www.livelearnstudy.net/

National Survey of Student Engagement. (n.d.). *Major Differences: Examining Student Engagement by Field of Study:Annual Results 2010*. Retrieved September 23, 2011, from National Survey of Student Engagement: http://nsse.iub.edu/NSSE_2010_Results/pdf/NSSE_2010_AnnualResults.pdf #page=44

NSSE. (2011). *Using NSSE Data*. Retrieved October 10, 2011, from National Survey of Student Engagement: http://nsse.iub.edu/2011_Institutional_Report/pdf/Using_NSSE_Data.pdf

Price, D. (2005, December). *Learning Communities and Student Success in Postsecondary Education: A Background Paper.* Retrieved September 23, 2010, from MDRC Organization: http://www.mdrc.org/publicatins/418/full.pdf

Rhoads, R. A. (1997). *Community Service and Higher Learning-Explorations of the Caring Self.* Albany: State University of New York Press.

Rudolph, F. (1990). *The American college and university: A history.* Athens: University of Georgia Press.

Schön, D. (1987). *Educating the Reflective Practitioner.* San Francisco: Jossey-Bass.

Schumaker, A., Reed, B. J., & Woods, S. (2000). "Collaborative models for metropolitan university outreach: The Omaha experience". *Cityscape. A Journal of Policy Development and Research,* 5(1), 197-207.

Seifer, S. D., & Vaughn, R. L. (2004). *Making a positive impact* (Report to the W.K. Kellogg Foundation). Seattle, WA: Community-Campus Partnerships for Health and the W.K. Kellogg Foundation.

Senior Learning Community. (n.d.). Retrieved March 19, 2009, from Wagner College: *http://www.wagner.edu/media/node/37*

Service-Learning Ideas and Curricular Examples. (n.d.). Retrieved March 19, 2009, from Learn and Serve America's National Service-Learning Clearninghouse: http://www.servicelearning.org/slice/index.php?ep_action=search

SIEDC to Announce St. George project with Wagner College. (2004, March 11). Staten Island Advance, p. A28.

Smith, B., MacGregor, J., Matthews, R., & Gabelnick, F. (2004). *Learning Communities: Reforming Undergraduate Education.* San Francisco: Jossey-Bass.

St. George Action Plan-A Civic Engagement Endeavor. (2004, April 27). Sixth Annual Staten Island Economic Development Conference, Staten Island, NY.

St. George Action Plan-A Civic Engagement Endeavor Symposium. (2004, April 20). Wagner College, Staten Island, NY.

Stiggins, R.J. (2005) *Assessment FOR Learning Defined.* Assessment Training Institute, in consultation with the team representing the United States at the ETS/Assessment Training Institute's International Conference: Promoting Sound Assessment in Every Classroom, Portland OR, September.

Students, W. B. (2004, March 10). SIED Partnership St. George Action Plan Press Conference. (S. I. Advance, Interviewer)

The National Task Force on Civic Learning and Democratic Engagement. (2012) *A Crucible Moment: College Learning and Democracy's Future.*Washington, DC: Association of American Colleges and Universities.

Tobolowsky, B. F. (2008). *Monograph #51: 2006 National Survey of First-Year Seminars: Continuing Innovations in the Collegiate Curriculum.* National Resource Center.

Tough, A. (1979). *The adult's learning projects* (2nd Ed.) Austin, TX: Learning Concepts. (The 1st edition, 1971, was published by the Ontario Institute for Studies in Education.)

Tucker, M.L., McCarthy, A.M., Hoxmeier, J.A. & Lenk, M.M., *Community Service-learning Increases Communication Skills across the Business Curriculum.* Business Communication Quarterly, Vol. 61(2), 1998, 88-99.

U.S. Department of Education, *A Test of Leadership: Charting the Future of U.S. Higher Education.* Washington, D.C., 2006. Retrieved September 25, 2011, from http://www2.ed.gov/about/bdscomm/list/hiedfuture/reports/pre-pub-report.pdf

Wagner College Business Team Up to Improve St. George. (2004, March 11). The Staten Island Advance, p. B4.

Wagner College Student Stephanie Bower Speaks about the St. George Action Plan. (2004, March 27). *Staten Island Advance, p. A9.*

Wagner College Students to Intern With Local Development Groups. (2005, March 23). The Staten Island Advance, p. A28.

Wagner College-Notable Program Activities:Campus, Classroom, and Community. (2005, April). The Periclean Progress E-Newsletter, Education & Citizenship, 1(5).

Washington Center for Improving the Quality of Undergraduate Education. (n.d.). Retrieved September 23, 2011, from National Learning Communities Directory: http://www.evergreen.edu/washcenter/directory.asp

Welhburg, C. M. (2011). "A Scholarly Approach to Assessing Learning". *International Journal for the Scholarship of Teaching and Learning,* July Vol. 5, No. 2.

What is Learn and Serve America? (n.d.). Retrieved August 1, 2009, from Learn & Serve America: http://www.learnandserve.gov

Worrall, L. (Fall 2007). "Asking the community: a case study of community partner perspectives". *Michigan Journal of Community Service-Learning*, 5-18.

www.ingramcontent.com/pod-product-compliance
Lightning Source LLC
Chambersburg PA
CBHW060420100426
42812CB00030B/3255/J